AMUSEMENT PARKS
of Pennsylvania

AMUSEMENT PARKS
of Pennsylvania

JIM FUTRELL

STACKPOLE
BOOKS

Published by
STACKPOLE BOOKS
5067 Ritter Road
Mechanicsburg, PA 17055
www.stackpolebooks.com

Printed in the United States of America

10 9 8 7 6 5 4 3 2 1

FIRST EDITION

Cover design by Wendy Reynolds
Photographs by the author, unless otherwise noted

Library of Congress Cataloging-in-Publication Data

Futrell, Jim.
    Amusement parks of Pennsylvania / Jim Futrell.–1st ed.
      p.   cm.
    Includes bibliographical references and index.
    ISBN 0-8117-2671-1
    1. Amusement parks–Pennsylvania–Guidebooks. 2. Amusement parks–Pennsylvania–History. I. Title: Amusement parks. II. Title.

GV1853.3.P46 F88   2002
791'.06'8–dc21

                                      2002019519

CONTENTS

FOREWORD

WHETHER YOU'RE RIDING THE CLASSIC BUMPER CARS AT KNOEBELS Amusement Resort, the vintage wooden coasters at Kennywood, or the Zephyr train at Dorney Park, nostalgia reigns at amusement parks from one end of Pennsylvania to another.

There's something special about the amusement parks in Pennsylvania. While corporate giants dominate park ownership throughout the country, the parks here are still mainly of the mom-and-pop variety. Sure, some are owned by big companies, but for some reason they don't have that big-company feel to them. If you're visiting a park in this state and you need to find top management or the owner, chances are you won't find him in his office. He's probably out sweeping up the midway, doing maintenance on a ride, or selling tickets at the front gate. In the amusement park world of today, that's unusual.

The parks of this state have a unique personality, and I think most of that comes from their history, their traditions, and the people who visit them. Adults living in this state are lucky. Little do they realize what they have. Parks have been a part of their summer routine for their entire lives, and residents of only a handful of states can lay claim to that distinction. People ask me why there is such a collection of great parks in Pennsylvania and Ohio, and why they continue to do so well year after year. The answer is simple: It's a tradition. My grandfather visited parks, and he took my father, who in turn took me, and now I'm taking my kids. It's a part of our lives. The parks are nearby, fun, clean, priced right, and have kept up with the times.

When Jim asked me to write the foreword to this book, I was delighted to be a small part of the project, because there isn't a person on earth more qualified to chronicle the history of Pennsylvania parks. He's more than a writer and historian. He probably knows more about the history of parks than anyone, and maybe most important of all, he's a passionate Pennsylvania parkie. If you invest time to read a book on this subject, you certainly want a man of his credentials to have written it.

Tim O'Brien
Parks and Attractions Editor
Amusement Business

ACKNOWLEDGMENTS

NO BOOK IS POSSIBLE WITHOUT THE SUPPORT OF NUMEROUS INDIVIDUALS. From the amusement parks themselves to their employees to the support and encouragement provided by friends, family, and coworkers, this book was the result of more than my efforts. Were it not for the generosity of the following people, this book would not have been possible.

This book started with Kyle Weaver of Stackpole Books, who developed the concept, contracted with me to be the author, and worked closely with me to guide me through the world of publishing and make this work a reality. His assistant, Amy Cooper, also deserves a thank-you for all her hard work.

I would also like to recognize two of the elder statesmen of the Pennsylvania amusement park industry, Robert Ott and Carl Hughes, who were more than generous in sharing their memories of their decades in the Pennsylvania amusement park industry, adding a special perspective to this book.

Individuals at Pennsylvania's amusement parks were also very cooperative, and I am certainly grateful for the assistance of the following: Ingrid and Morgan Hughes of Williams Grove Amusement Park; Jerome Gibas of Idlewild Park; Mark Sosnowski of Dorney Park; Gene Rumsey of Conneaut Lake Community Park; Barry Kumpf of Lakemont Park; Paul Nelson and Steve Gorman of Waldameer Park; Mary Lou Rosemeyer of Kennywood; Neal Fehnel and Ron Long of Bushkill Park; Kathy Burrows of Hersheypark; Peter Gardella and Murf DelGrosso of DelGrosso's Amusement Park; Dick Knoebel and Joe Muscato of Knoebels Amusement Resort; Murl Clark and Gary Chubb of Dutch Wonderland; Audrey

Shapiro of Sesame Place; Steve Bender of Weona Park; Joe Pandolfo at Pocono Play Park; Sandy Hawkins of Land of Little Horses; Richard Franks of Bucktail Camping Resort; Sam Willard of Carousel Village at Indian Walk; and Richard Fritz and Marty Hennis of Dandy's Frontier.

Also of great assistance were three historians, each with his own special expertise. Thank-you to Charles Jacques, for sharing his knowledge of amusement park history; Paul Korol, for his study of the history of Pennsylvania; and Stan Baker, for his research on Capt. Paul Boyton, the inventor of the modern amusement park.

Thanks are also due my friends and family for all of their support during the two-year process of making this book a reality, especially my sister Mary, for her editing expertise.

One person, more than any other, deserves my special gratitude for making this book a reality—my wife and best friend, Marlowe. She shares and appreciates my passion for amusement parks, and despite what she knew would be a difficult and time-consuming effort, she never wavered in her support and provided the foundation on which to write this book. I will always remember that, and I dedicate this book to her.

I also hope that my two boys, Jimmy and Christopher, will look back fondly on the summer of 2000 as the year they got to visit every amusement park in the state of Pennsylvania. Thanks for the memories.

INTRODUCTION

IN THIS ERA OF THE HOMOGENOUS MASS-PRODUCED CHAINS, MOST OF US have come to appreciate the one-of-a-kind, family-owned business. Be it a diner, a bed and breakfast, a meat market, or that special clothing store around the corner, these businesses tend to stand out in today's fast-paced era.

The amusement park industry is no different. While the huge corporate-owned theme parks dominate the industry, the family-owned park is still alive and well, and no state has a higher concentration of them than Pennsylvania. Of the eighteen parks profiled in this book, just five are not owned by a family. What is even more remarkable is that eight of them have been in operation for over one hundred years. They are not just businesses, they are cherished family heirlooms, which gives each one its own personality.

Because of this legacy, each of Pennsylvania's amusement parks—large or small, family, community, or corporate owned—has a special story behind it, representing the dreams and hard work of generations of individuals. I have tried to convey those stories so that you can truly appreciate each park's unique personality when you visit.

Before you venture out, here are a few general tips to make your day more enjoyable:

- *Dress comfortably.* Make sure you wear comfortable shoes that are broken in. Wear cool, loose-fitting clothes, but not too loose, as they might get caught on something. Take along a jacket and a rain poncho, just in case.

- *Pack lightly.* You're going to be walking around all day, so don't weigh yourself down with a lot of stuff. Most parks have lockers at the front entrance where you can store things you might need during the day.

- *Eat a good breakfast.* Arriving at the park hungry means that you might waste time that could otherwise be spent riding. Don't stuff yourself with greasy food, however, which doesn't mix well with rides.

- *Arrive early.* Typically the best time of day at an amusement park is the first hour it's open, before the bulk of the people show up. This is often the best time to ride some of the big rides.

- *Hit the big rides first.* While most visitors tend to rush to the big rides first, the lines will only increase as the day wears on, although they usually grow shorter in the evening, when the roller coasters tend to be running faster. Try to avoid the big rides between noon and 5 P.M.

- *Follow the rules.* All parks have rules and regulations and set height limits for certain rides and attractions. A great deal of thought has gone into developing these rules and limits, and they are there to protect you. Please respect them. Also note that in the state of Pennsylvania, a rider responsibility act requires customers to follow posted ruled and regulations.

One of the great things about amusement parks is that they are constantly evolving and changing. While every effort had been made to ensure the accuracy of this book, some changes may have occurred. Please call ahead to confirm admission policies and operating hours.

A History of
the Amusement
Park Industry

HUMAN BEINGS ARE, BY NATURE, SOCIAL CREATURES. SINCE THE BEGIN-
ning of time, people have sought ways to come together and escape the
pressures of everyday life. As humankind started to settle in villages,
festivals and celebrations became a popular way for the community to
relax. As villages grew into cities, parcels of land were set aside as sort
of a permanent festival. In medieval Europe, these places were known
as pleasure gardens.

In the 1500s and 1600s, pleasure gardens sprang up on the outskirts
of major cities. At a time when Europe's cities were crowded, dirty, dis-
ease-ridden places, these pleasure gardens provided a welcome respite.
In many ways, they were similar to today's amusement parks, offering
landscaped gardens, live entertainment, fireworks, dancing, games, and
even primitive amusement rides, including the forerunners of today's
merry-go-rounds, Ferris wheels, and roller coasters.

Pleasure gardens remained extremely popular until the late 1700s,
when political unrest and urban sprawl caused a decline that lasted
until the mid-1800s. While most of the pleasure gardens are now faded
memories, two still exist. Dyrehavs Bakken, which opened in 1583 outside Copenhagen, Denmark, is the world's oldest operating amusement
park, and the Prater in Vienna, which got its start in 1766 when the
emperor turned a portion of his private hunting preserve over to public
amusement, is now a beloved Viennese tradition.

Coming to America

As the pleasure garden was dying out in Europe, a new nation, the United States, was growing into a world power. Immigrants flocking to cities such as New York, Philadelphia, and Boston clamored for recreation. Entrepreneurs responded by developing picnic groves and beer gardens throughout America.

Jones Woods, widely accepted as America's first large amusement resort, opened along the East River in New York in the early 1800s. Its attractions included bowling, billiards, gymnasium equipment, a shooting gallery, donkey rides, music, dancing, and a beer garden. Jones Woods' popularity was short-lived, however, as the rapid growth of Manhattan soon overtook the resort.

The continuing demand for amusement in New York was soon answered on a peninsula in Brooklyn, New York, known as Coney Island, named for the coneys, or wild rabbits, that inhabited the area. The seaside location provided a cool getaway in the hot summer months, and in 1829, a hotel catering to visitors appeared on the sands. By the early 1850s, pavilions offering bathing, dining, and dancing were being constructed at Coney Island. Around 1875, a railroad to the resort was completed, and the destination's popularity quickly increased. Entrepreneurs responded by opening cabarets, vaudeville theaters, fortune-telling booths, games, and rides such as small carousels. Here in 1867, a creative restaurateur, named Charles Feltman, invented the hot dog. The resort's first major amusement device opened in 1877 when the 300-foot-tall Iron Tower, a star attraction of the 1876 Centennial Exposition in Philadelphia, was relocated to the resort. Just seven years later, in 1884, the modern roller coaster was invented when La Marcus Thompson built the Switchback Railroad along the seashore. Throughout its history, however, Coney Island was never an amusement park, but a neighborhood in Brooklyn that featured a collection of amusements, including several independent amusement parks.

Early amusement resort growth was not confined to New York. In 1846, large crowds gathered at a family farm in Bristol, Connecticut, to view a failed science experiment. The size of the crowd convinced the farm's owner, Gad Norton, that there was a big need for a recreational gathering place in central Connecticut. Norton converted his farm into an amusement resort called Lake Compounce, where people could enjoy picnicking, boating in the lake, listening to band concerts, and dancing. Today Lake Compounce continues as the oldest operating amusement park in the United States. Another early amusement resort, called Rocky Point Park, opened nearby in Warwick, Rhode Island, in 1847. This seaside resort continued to operate until 1995.

In the years following the Civil War, the personality of the country changed as America's cities became increasingly crowded and industrialized. Farmers flocked to the cities to find jobs in the new factories. The growing congestion encouraged many to seek out recreation away from the cities. Many amusement resorts opened along the ocean shore or by a lake, where people could find a cool getaway in the hot summer. But the primary engine for the development of the amusement park in America was the trolley company.

In the wake of the opening of the first practical electric-powered street rail line in Richmond, Virginia, in 1888, hundreds of trolley lines popped up around the country almost overnight. At that time, utility companies charged the trolley companies a flat fee for the use of their electricity. The transportation companies looked for a way to stimulate weekend ridership to make the most of their investment. Opening amusement resorts provided the ideal solution. Typically built at the end of the trolley lines, these resorts initially were simple operations consisting of picnic facilities, dance halls, restaurants, games, and a few amusement rides. These parks were immediately successful and soon opened across America.

Becoming an American Institution

The amusement park became an institution in the wake of the 1893 World's Columbian Exposition in Chicago. This world's fair introduced the Ferris wheel and the amusement midway to the world. The midway, essentially a long walkway lined with a wide array of rides and concessions, was a huge success and set the precedent for amusement park design for the next sixty years.

The following year, Capt. Paul Boyton borrowed the midway concept and opened the world's first modern amusement park, Paul Boyton's Water Chutes, on Chicago's South Side. Boyton was a colorful figure who served in the Union navy during the Civil War and fought in the Franco-Prussian War. In 1874, he stowed away on an ocean liner with the intent of jumping overboard 200 miles out to sea to test an "unsinkable" rubber lifesaving suit. He was apprehended but was eventually permitted by the captain to jump overboard 30 miles off the coast of Ireland. Boyton safely made it to land, achieving international fame. He followed that accomplishment by becoming the first person to swim the English Channel. In 1888, he settled in Chicago, where he started an aquatic circus and raised sea lions in Lake Michigan. Soon he came across a Shoot the Chutes water ride in Rock Island, Illinois, where it had recently been invented in 1889. Boyton was intrigued by the simple ride, in which a boat traveled down an inclined plane into a body of water. This was the first major water-based amusement ride and the forerunner of today's

SHOOTING THE CHUTES.

Capt. Paul Boyton's Water Chutes was the first amusement park in which rides were the main attraction. AUTHOR'S COLLECTION

log flumes and splash-down rides. Boyton purchased the rights to Shoot the Chutes and tested it in London in 1893 before setting it up in Chicago as the centerpiece of his new park.

Unlike the primitive trolley parks, which were just starting to come into their own, Boyton's Water Chutes was the first amusement park to charge admission and use rides as its main draw, rather than picnic facilities or a natural feature such as a beach or a lake. Patrons from all over Chicago flocked to Captain Boyton's operation to ride the 60-foot-tall Water Chutes. Over five hundred thousand people showed up in that first season alone. Boyton's park relocated to a larger site in 1896, but it closed in 1908, eclipsed by larger and more modern facilities. However, the success of his Chicago park inspired him to open a similar facility, Sea Lion Park, at the fledgling Coney Island resort in New York in 1895. The park featured not only a water chute ride, but also the Flip Flap, one of the first looping roller coasters, and a sea lion show that foreshadowed those at today's theme parks.

Sea Lion Park was Coney Island's first true amusement park—a collection of rides and shows in a fenced area for which patrons paid admission. With the opening of Sea Lion Park, Coney Island became the center of the amusement universe. Entrepreneurs from all over flocked to develop new rides and attractions for the masses. George Tilyou, a successful Coney Island restaurant operator, opened Steeplechase Park in 1897. The park, with its well-manicured gardens, took amusement to a whole new level. Soon the park became internationally renowned for its signature Steeplechase ride, which allowed patrons to experience the thrills of a horse race by riding wooden horses along eight parallel, undulating tracks.

The success of Steeplechase Park hurt business at Sea Lion Park, and in 1902, Boyton sold the struggling operation to businessmen Frederick Thompson and Elmer Dundy, who had found fame at the Pan American Exposition in Buffalo, New York, in 1901, when they introduced their successful Trip to the Moon, one of the first simulator attractions. After moving it to Steeplechase Park, where they operated it as a concession for the 1902 season, they wanted to set out on their own. The result of this ambition was Luna Park, reportedly named after Dundy's sister. Described in advertisements as "an electric Eden unlike anything that had ever been built before," it was characterized by its fanciful "Arabian Nights" style of architecture outlined by 250,000 electric lights. At a time when electrical lighting was rare in most houses, Luna Park created a sensation, attracting over forty thousand patrons at its opening in May 1903.

Luna Park represented a new genre of amusement park known as the exposition park, which looked to the Chicago World's Fair for inspiration. These parks featured elaborate buildings with fanciful designs highlighted by thousands of electric lights. There were attractions that were considered very complex for their time, such as re-creations of famous

Coney Island's Luna Park was the first exposition park. AUTHOR'S COLLECTION

disasters, scaled-down replicas of distant lands, and displays of prematurely born infants being cared for with technology so advanced that hospitals had yet to install it. Unlike the more pastoral trolley parks, exposition parks tended to be raucous, packed with attractions, and located close to the urban center. Among the more famous exposition parks were White City in Chicago (opened in 1905); Luna Park in Pittsburgh (1905); Luna Park in Cleveland (1905); and Wonderland near Boston (1906). While most larger cities featured an exposition park, the phenomenon was largely short-lived because of high overhead and the high cost of the new attractions they added. However, one remains in operation: Lakeside Park in Denver, which opened as White City in 1908 and still features its elaborate Tower of Jewels.

Perhaps the grandest exposition park of them all was Dreamland, which opened across the street from Coney Island's Luna Park in 1904. Dreamland tried to top Luna Park in every respect. At the center of the park was a 375-foot-tall tower, the buildings were outlined with a million electric lights, and the entire place was adorned with elaborate facades, fountains, pools, and floral displays. Among the attractions were Lilliputia, a complete city populated by three hundred little people, and the huge Fighting the Flames show, which claimed to have a cast of four thousand. With the opening of Dreamland, Coney Island was at its zenith,

with three immense amusement parks and dozens of individual concessions catering to the millions that flocked there. Steeplechase's Tilyou was quoted as stating, "If Paris is France, then Coney Island between May and September is the world."

Even a fire at Steeplechase Park in 1907 that burnt the park to the ground failed to put a damper on things. After charging customers 10 cents a head to view the "burning ruins," owner George Tilyou immediately rebuilt the park bigger and better than ever. The Steeplechase

Dreamland at Coney Island was the largest and most spectacular exposition park. AUTHOR'S COLLECTION

After it burned to the ground in 1907, Steeplechase Park was rebuilt with the Pavilion of Fun as its centerpiece. It was demolished in 1966. AUTHOR'S COLLECTION

ride remained and encircled the Pavilion of Fun, a 5-acre building featuring rides and fun house devices.

Unfortunately, fire became a constant nemesis of Coney Island, with twenty major conflagrations striking the resort area through its history. The largest completely destroyed Dreamland as it was preparing for the 1911 season. Never as successful as Luna Park or Steeplechase, it was not rebuilt, although other amusement attractions soon moved in on the ruins to take Dreamland's place. The destruction of Dreamland signified the beginning of Coney Island's slow decline, however. The following year, Luna Park went bankrupt but managed to hold on until 1944, when it too was done in by fire. Steeplechase closed in 1964 and sat abandoned for two years before being demolished. Into the 1980s, many of Coney Island's remaining landmarks succumbed—the once-great restaurants and bathhouses, and three of its greatest roller coasters, the Bobsled in 1974, the Tornado in 1977, and the Thunderbolt in 1982. Although only a fraction of its original size, Coney Island has hung on, and is enjoying a renewed appreciation with its surviving vintage attractions, such as the 1920 Wonder Wheel and the 1927 Cyclone roller coaster, both now listed as national landmarks.

The success of Coney Island during the early part of the twentieth century helped spread the amusement park industry throughout the country. Trolley companies, breweries, and entrepreneurs opened parks by the hundreds. The number of operating parks grew from approximately 250 in 1899 to nearly 700 in 1905. By 1919, over 1,500 amusement parks were in operation in the United States. In 1913, *World's Work* magazine described the growth as "a hysteria of parks followed by a panic." *Billboard* magazine sounded a cautionary message in 1909: "The great profits made by some of the park men produce a mania for park building, which can well be compared to some of the booms in mining camps. Men from almost all professions of life flocked to this endeavor, and without knowledge or particular ability in this line endeavored to build parks." Soon every major city had at least one major park.

Amusement parks during this time had a much different personality than they do today. A review of the industry by *Billboard* magazine in 1905 summed up the keys to a successful attraction as "plenty of shade, attractive landscaping, sufficient transportation, first class attractions (live entertainment) and a variety of good up to date privileges," as rides and concessions were then known. Rides were almost an afterthought in the article and only mentioned after an in-depth discussion of the importance of a summer theater, presenting summer stock, vaudeville, and concerts, which it considered to be the heart of the park. But that personality would soon change.

The Golden Age

With amusement parks opening at such a rapid pace in the early twentieth century, patrons were looking for more thrilling attractions, and soon a whole new industry sprang up to fulfill this need. The William F. Mangels Company was founded at Coney Island in 1890 and in 1914 introduced the whip, one of the first mass-produced rides. The Eli Bridge Company started operations in 1900 and to this day continues to manufacture the Ferris wheels that are a midway staple. Other companies founded during this period include the Philadelphia Toboggan Company, one of the largest manufacturers of roller coasters and carousels, which started making rides in 1904. In 1912, the Dayton Fun House Company was formed. This company was the forerunner to National Amusement Devices and, later, International Amusement Devices, one of the largest and most prolific builders of amusement rides before folding in the mid-1980s. The Dodgem Corporation opened in 1919 in Salisbury Beach, Massachusetts, introducing bumper cars to amusement parks.

In the competition to sell the most rides, innovation was the watchword. Riverview Park in Chicago built a roller coaster called the Potsdam Railway in 1908, in which the cars were suspended beneath the track rather than riding above it. In 1912, John Miller, the most prolific ride builder of this era, patented a system of holding a roller coaster to the track that remains in use to this day. This new system, called under-friction, made it impossible for roller coasters to leave the tracks, for-ever changing the nature of roller coasters from mild-mannered scenic railways to true thrillers.

New technology such as the wide-scale rollout of underfriction roller coasters converged with the booming economy and the newfound popu-larity of the automobile in the 1920s to propel the amusement park industry into its Golden Age. As most trolley companies had long since divested their amusement park operations, a whole new generation of entrepreneurs flocked to the industry, building amusement parks that catered to the automobile trade. The automobile led to the closing of dozens of smaller amusement parks throughout the country that were unable to provide large parking lots, but the surviving parks boomed, and thrill rides were the primary draw. America was in a mood to play, and there was an insatiable demand for thrills and entertainment at America's amusement parks.

Business continued booming through the 1920s, and amusement parks were constantly looking for new ways to thrill patrons. Roller coasters became larger and more thrilling, and every year a new ride was introduced to the masses. The Tumble Bug, a large ride featuring cars traveling along a circular undulating track, immediately became a favorite upon its invention in 1925. The Tilt-A-Whirl was introduced to the midway in 1926. In 1928, Leon Cassidy constructed the first rail-guided "dark ride," which took patrons through a darkened building to view various scenes, at Tumbling Run Park, Bridgewater, New Jersey, leading to the formation of the Pretzel Amusement Company, a major manufacturer of dark rides. Inspired by the Winter Olympic bobsled tracks, Norman Bartlett introduced the Flying Turns, a roller coaster in which trains traveled down a trough rather than on tracks, in 1929 at Lakeside Park, Dayton, Ohio.

Enterprising businessmen were not the only ones getting involved in the industry. In 1928, Westchester County, New York, recognizing the value of having a recreational community gathering place, acquired a collection of ramshackle amusements along the shores of Long Island Sound and replaced them with Playland. Unlike most amusement parks of the era, which had gradually evolved over several decades, West-chester County carefully laid out Playland to provide the optimal mix of rides and attractions. This precise planning was a predecessor to the design of the large corporate theme parks that would open three decades later. The main attractions were arranged around a lushly landscaped mall, and the kiddie attractions were located in a separate small area. In addition to the park's main roller coaster, the Aeroplane, a milder ride,

The original layout from 1928 of Playland in Rye, New York, was so successful that it has changed little since.

the Dragon Coaster, was located just across the midway. Recreation attractions such as an ice rink, swimming pool, beach, and nature preserve complemented the amusements, and a large parking lot accommodated the growing number of automobiles. Towering above it all was the music tower, which broadcast peaceful music throughout the park. People flocked to the facility, with attendance the first season reaching 2.8 million. The basic design of Playland has changed little to this day, although many of the rides and attractions have been updated to appeal to new generations.

Hard Times

As Playland was setting new design standards for the amusement park industry, the stock market crash of 1929 drove America into the Great Depression. With unemployment peaking at 33 percent, consumers had little money to spend on entertainment, let alone a day at an amusement park. The Depression took a horrible toll on the industry, and hundreds of parks closed across the country. By 1935, only four hundred amusement parks remained open. With capital virtually nonexistent, parks did whatever it took to hang on. Popular strategies to attract crowds included food giveaways and live entertainment, or "flesh shows," as they were known. Not all was bleak, as this became the golden age of big bands, which toured amusement parks from coast to coast. The crowds that big bands attracted to many amusement parks were credited with saving dozens of amusement parks during the 1930s.

Fortunately, things did improve, and amusement parks slowly started to get back on track by the late 1930s. Long-deferred maintenance was done, and new attractions were added. But dark clouds were looming on the horizon once again. In late 1941, America entered World War II, and soon the resources of the nation were focused on the war effort.

The war was a mixed blessing for the amusement park industry. On one hand, with the economy booming in support of the war effort, patrons flocked to amusement parks located near industrial centers and military installations, providing a much-needed cash infusion for the parks. At the same time, gasoline rationing severely hindered operation at parks not easily reached by public transportation. In fact, many parks closed for the duration of the war and in some cases never reopened. Also, with the nation's industrial output fully focused on wartime production, amusement parks could not add new rides, and material shortages made maintenance on existing rides difficult.

When World War II finally ended, America and the amusement park industry enjoyed a period of postwar prosperity. Attendance and revenues grew to record levels, and new parks opened across America. But the world was a rapidly changing place. Veterans sought to capture their portion of the American dream and start families. Many flocked to the suburbs.

When it opened in 1925, San Antonio's Kiddie Park was the first amusement park especially for kids and foreshadowed the kiddieland boom three decades later.

Entrepreneurs reacted by developing a new concept that soon became as much of a fixture in suburbia as the tract home—the "kiddieland," a special amusement park featuring rides just for kids. The concept had actually been developed in 1925, when C. C. Macdonald opened the Kiddie Park in San Antonio, Texas, which remains in operation. Kiddielands grew from fewer than two dozen in 1950 to more than 150 operating throughout the country by 1960. They were located primarily in large cities such as New York, Chicago, and Los Angeles. Even the primary monument to suburbia, the shopping center, got into the act as several constructed their own kiddielands, with the first opening at Northgate Mall in Seattle in 1950. The kiddieland boom was short-lived. Rising property values and an aging target market shut down most of the kiddielands by the late 1960s. Though some grew into full-fledged amusement parks, fewer than a dozen from this era still remain in operation, including Pixie Playland, Concord, California; Funland, Idaho Falls, Idaho; Hoffman's Playland, Latham, New York; and Memphis Kiddie Park, outside Cleveland.

As America was flocking to the suburbs, the core of the industry, the large urban amusement park, was being left behind in the face of aging infrastructure, television, urban decay, and desegregation. Coming off the capital constraints of the Great Depression and World War II, many parks were struggling to become updated and stay competitive. It seemed that these parks were becoming increasingly irrelevant, as the public turned elsewhere for entertainment. What was needed was a new concept to reignite the industry, and that new concept was Disneyland.

The Theme Park Era

By the 1950s, Walt Disney was an internationally renowned filmmaker. He often spent Sunday afternoons with his kids at a local amusement park, lamenting the fact that there was nothing that the family could enjoy together. Disney initially considered building a small entertainment facility at his movie studio, featuring a train, boat and stagecoach rides, a Wild West town, and a circus. But as his dream grew, so did the size of the project.

When Disneyland first opened in 1955 on a former orange grove in Anaheim, California, many people were skeptical that an amusement park without any of the traditional attractions would succeed. There were no roller coasters, no swimming pool or beach, and no midway games. Instead of a midway, Disneyland offered five distinct themed areas—Main Street, Adventureland, Frontierland, Fantasyland, and Tomorrowland—providing guests with the fantasy of travel to different lands and times. Disneyland was an immediate success, attracting nearly 4 million people in its first year of operation. The theme park era was born.

Opened in 1955, Disneyland, in Anaheim, California, set off the theme park era.

Robert Ott, former chairman of Dorney Park in Allentown, Pennsylvania, credits Disney with changing many things: "the way parks are organized, cleanliness, the use of lights and colors. He catered to the customers, made them happy. His magic flowed into amusement parks. We all benefited from it." Carl Hughes, chairman of Kennywood, one of America's best remaining traditional parks, concurs: "The standards changed. You couldn't get away with dirty midways and surly employees." It was a whole new era for the amusement park industry.

While Disneyland is often given credit for being the first theme park, the concept had actually been evolving for more than a decade before Disneyland, as several smaller attractions opened that embraced a single theme. Many of these attractions, which helped inspire Disney, are still in operation today. These include Knott's Berry Farm in Buena Park, California, which started building its Ghost Town in 1940; Holiday World (originally Santa Claus Land), which opened in 1946 in Santa Claus, Indiana; Santa's Workshop, North Pole, New York, which started in 1949; Paul Bunyan Center, which opened in Brainerd, Minnesota, in 1950; and Great Escape (formerly Storytown USA) in Lake George, New York, which first welcomed visitors in 1954.

As important as the opening of Disneyland was, Ott remembers another event that was also important in changing the face of the industry in the 1950s. In 1958, the industry trade association, then known as the National Association of Amusement Parks, Pools and Beaches, took a tour of Europe. Since the European industry was largely wiped out during World War II, it had been rebuilding with a level of sophistication not yet found in American parks—intricate flowerbeds, elaborate landscaping, and flashy new rides adorned with thousands of electric lights. "That trip changed the industry," Ott recalled. "We brought back new and more sophisticated ideas." While these new ideas created an even more sophisticated industry in America, implementing them was quite expensive. For parks struggling to come back from the Depression and World War II, it was too much.

The excitement created by Disneyland and the ideas from Europe opened a new era for amusement parks, but the industry suffered some growing pains. A variety of parks attempted to cash in on Disney's concept, but many lacked the appeal of Disney or simply did not have the financial resources. In 1958, Magic Mountain opened west of Denver when it was only partially completed, and it closed almost immediately. It later reopened and now exists as a shopping village with a few rides. Pacific Ocean Park, widely credited with making the pay-one-price admission an industry standard, opened in Ocean Park, California, in 1958 with the backing of CBS, but it collapsed under high maintenance bills in 1968. Pleasure Island debuted near Boston in 1959, but it could never get its main attraction, a giant robotic replica of Moby Dick that was supposed to rear out of a body of water, to work properly. It closed in 1969, never achieving its hoped-for popularity. But the most spectacular failure was Freedomland in the Bronx. Built in the shape of the United States, the park opened in 1960, incomplete and overbudget. From the beginning, it was plagued by accidents, poorly planned attractions, insufficient capacity, and a robbery. Furthermore, the park was constructed atop a former landfill on improperly graded land. The buildings shifted as they settled and required expensive repairs. It struggled on until 1964, when it collapsed under a mountain of debt.

It wasn't until 1961, when Six Flags Over Texas opened between Dallas and Fort Worth, that another major theme park was finally successful. Backed by the land development firm Great Southwest Corporation, the park was the first in what today is the largest theme park chain in the world. Six Flags adapted traditional amusement park rides to a theme park, introducing the log flume to the industry in 1963 and building the first Runaway Mine Train roller coaster in 1966.

Following on the success of Six Flags, which proved that the theme park was a viable concept apart from Disney, theme park development during this time took off. Between 1964 and early 1965, fifteen theme parks opened, and *Amusement Business* reported that twenty additional projects were in the works. While these tended to be smaller, short-lived roadside attractions, the success of Six Flags had caught the attention of major corporations, such as Clairol, Penn Central, ABC, Marriott, Taft Broadcasting, and Mattel, which were soon planning their own parks. Even Bob Hope considered opening a theme park in Los Angeles in the 1960s. Among the major parks opening during this time were the first Sea World theme park, which debuted in San Diego in 1964; Six Flags Over Georgia in Atlanta in 1967; Astroworld in Houston in 1968; Magic Mountain near Los Angeles, Six Flags Over Mid-America outside St. Louis, and the immense Walt Disney World in Florida, all in 1971; and Opryland in Nashville in 1972. What these parks had in common was a location close to interstate highways on the outskirts of town, high standards of design and operation, and disdain for traditional amusement park attractions such as wooden roller coasters and midway games.

That disdain, however, changed in 1972 when Taft Broadcasting opened Kings Island near Cincinnati. Kings Island was different from most theme parks. Its roots were found in a very successful traditional amusement park—Coney Island in Cincinnati—which had been regarded as one of the most successful and best-run amusement parks in the country. Walt Disney even visited Coney Island to observe its operations while planning for Disneyland. Its popularity was a double-edged sword, however, because it became increasingly difficult to accommodate growing crowds in its cramped location on the Ohio River. In addition, flooding was a constant nuisance. As a result, in 1969 it was decided to relocate the park to a larger site in the suburbs, where it would become a major theme park. Given Coney Island's success, its owners had no reservations about including traditional amusement park attractions, even persuading renowned roller coaster designer John Allen to come out of retirement and build two wooden roller coasters—the twin-track Racer and the smaller Scooby Doo (now the Beastie). The new park was called Kings Island.

People flocked to Kings Island and lined up for hours to ride the Racer. Kings Island proved that people were still longing for traditional thrills, and the industry responded by opening more theme parks. In 1973, Carowinds opened near Charlotte, followed by Great Adventure in New Jersey and Kings Dominion in Richmond in 1974; Busch Gardens Williamsburg in Virginia in 1975; and Minneapolis's Valleyfair and the

The Racer at Kings Island, outside Cincinnati, introduced the wooden roller coaster to the theme park.

two Great America parks in California and Illinois in 1976. While these parks continued to embrace many of the design standards of their earlier cousins, their resistance to more traditional amusement park rides was not as strong as had been the case with their predecessors.

Trying to Compete

While theme parks increasingly dominated the industry in the 1960s and 1970s, the old traditional parks were facing hard times. Several factors made it difficult for many parks to compete in this new climate. Aging rides and buildings were in need of upgrades, and the increasing sophistication of attractions at the theme parks made new attractions increasingly expensive to purchase and maintain. The congested urban location of many older parks made expansion difficult, and urban decay often caused the loss of family business. Finally, increasing land values prompted many park operators to sell their facilities to developers. As a result, the industry saw the sad closing of many large urban traditional parks—parks that used to be the cornerstones of the industry.

Not all was bleak, however. Many traditional amusement parks learned from theme parks and revitalized their operations. Hersheypark in Pennsylvania revived its business by adding a series of themed areas. Other parks such as Kennywood in West Mifflin, Pennsylvania, maintained their traditional atmosphere but incorporated ideas pioneered by theme parks, including uniformed employees, live entertainment, costumed characters, and theme-park-style rides such as log flumes, observation towers, and monorails.

Competition and New Concepts

Theme park development had slowed dramatically by the late 1970s, simply because most of the markets large enough to support such a facility now had a park. As a result, most theme park operators concentrated on expanding and improving existing facilities. Most attention was focused on topping one another with record-breaking roller coasters. Sparked by the interest generated by Kings Island's Racer, the seventies saw a roller coaster arms race. New record-breaking heights were achieved, and in 1975, Knott's Berry Farm and Arrow Development Corporation built a steel Corkscrew looping roller coaster. Soon looping roller coasters were must-have attractions for successful theme parks. The intense competition sparked innovations in ride technology, which reached a level of complexity never before experienced. Most rides were now computer controlled and made by new high-tech manufacturing processes.

Chicago's Riverview was one of the greatest urban traditional parks to close in the 1960s. AUTHOR'S COLLECTION

This was all very expensive, and rapidly increasing manufacturing costs, coupled with a downturn in the industrial economy, which provided the picnic business that so many traditional parks relied upon, brought about another wave of park closures in the late 1970s. By the end of the decade, nearly one hundred amusement parks had closed forever.

As the industry entered the 1980s, opportunities for new theme parks were limited, and the demand for large thrill rides was waning, with an aging population and increasing costs. The popularity of water attractions skyrocketed during this decade, however, as they could be enjoyed by the entire family and provided a fun way to cool off on a hot summer day. New concepts included the river rapids (introduced in 1980), the splashwater (1984), and the "dry" water slide (1986). It was an era of tremendous growth for water parks, which eschewed traditional rides for water slides. The first water park, Wet 'n Wild, opened in Orlando in 1977, but the concept truly took off in the 1980s. In 1983, Geauga Lake in Aurora, Ohio, became the first amusement park to add a full-scale water park to its lineup of traditional amusement park attractions.

The ride simulator was another attraction that many amusement parks thought would be the wave of the future during the 1980s. Small versions such as the Astroliner had been available since 1978, but the opening of Star Tours at Disneyland in 1987 took the experience to an entirely new level. Industry observers predicted that simulators would supplant traditional thrill rides, because they could easily be reprogrammed into a new ride experience every few years. Most major theme parks added a simulator, but the lines at the roller coasters did not grow any shorter.

Many American theme park operators also turned their attention overseas. Disney became the first major American operator to do so, opening Tokyo Disneyland in Japan in 1985. It soon became the world's most popular amusement park and set off a wave of theme park construction in Asia, turning it into the second-largest amusement park market in the world.

The Industry Today

By the late 1980s, amusement park operators realized something very surprising: As the "baby boom" generation got older, they were not retiring from enjoying thrill rides as previous generations had done. The roller coaster innovations in the late 1970s failed to satiate their appetite for thrills, and in 1988, the arms race began anew with the construction of the 170-foot-tall Shock Wave at Six Flags Great America in Gurnee, Illinois. It held the record for only a year, however. The following season, Cedar Point in Sandusky, Ohio, constructed the Magnum XL 200, the first roller coaster to surpass 200 feet in height. The arms race contin-

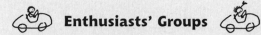

Enthusiasts' Groups

There are dozens of organizations for people interested in amusement parks or in specific rides. The largest of these are listed here.

American Carousel Society

3845 Telegraph Rd.
Elkton, MD 21921-2442

www.carousel.org/acs/

Membership includes three newsletters, a convention summary newsletter, a biennial census of operating wooden carousels, a membership directory, and convention materials.

American Coaster Enthusiasts (ACE)

5800 Foxridge Dr.
Suite 115
Mission, KS 66202-2333

www.aceonline.com

Publications include the quarterly magazine *Roller Coaster!* and *ACE News*, a bimonthly newsletter. ACE usually hosts five events a year in North America.

Dark Ride and Fun House Enthusiasts

P.O. Box 484
Vienna, OH 44473-0484

www.dafe.org

Publishes *Barrel of Fun*, a quarterly newsletter, and hosts at least one event a year.

The Dark Ride and Fun House Historical Society

22 Cozzens Ave.
Highland Falls, NY 10928

www.laffinthedark.com

Features on-line newsletter.

European Coaster Club

Six Green Lane
Hillingdon, Middlesex
UB8 3EB England

www.coasterclub.org

Publishes *First Drop*, a bimonthly magazine, and hosts six to eight events a year, usually in Europe.

(continued on page 20)

Enthusiasts' Groups
(continued from page 19)

National Amusement Park Historical Association (NAPHA)

P.O. Box 83
Mount Prospect, IL 60056

www.napha.org

The only club following all aspects of the amusement
and theme park industry. Publishes *NAPHA News*,
a bimonthly magazine, and the monthly newsletter
NAPHA NewsFLASH!!! Hosts two to four events
annually, primarily in North America.

National Carousel Association

P.O. Box 4333
Evansville, IN 47724-0333

www.carousel.org/nca/

Membership benefits include the quarterly magazine
Merry-Go-Roundup, a biennial census report of existing
carousels, and a biennial membership listing. Hosts
an annual convention and a technical conference.

Roller Coaster Club of Great Britain (RCCGB)

P.O. Box 235
Uxbridge, Middlesex UB10 0TF
England

www.rccgb.co.uk

Publishes *Airtime*, a bimonthly newsletter,
and a yearbook. Hosts six to eight events a year,
primarily in Europe.

Additionally, a wealth of clubs around the world target specific regions or interests. These include Coaster Enthusiasts of Canada, Coaster Riders of America, Coaster Zombies, Florida Coaster Club, Freundeskreis Freizeitparks (Germany), Great Ohio Coaster Club, Kentucky Coaster Club, Mid Atlantic Coaster Club, Pennsylvania Park and Coaster Club, Rollercoaster Friends (Belgium), Western New York Coaster Club, and WildWest Coaster Club.

ues unabated to this day, and in the year 2000, about a hundred roller coasters opened around the world, including the new world's record for the largest and fastest roller coaster, the Steel Dragon at Nagashima Spaland in Japan, at 318 feet tall and 95 miles per hour.

The year 1988 was also significant in that the development of new theme parks in the United States resumed, some being built in cities that had once been considered too small for such an attraction.

In the 1990s, the amusement park industry enjoyed a level of prosperity not seen since the 1920s. Theme parks were opening around the world and attracting record numbers of people. Although some parks did close, the traditional parks that survived the hard times have learned to compete and have become beloved local institutions.

The distinction between theme and traditional parks has become blurred, with theme parks adding thrill rides that have little connection to their original themes and traditional parks adding themed areas. And the two have always shared a desire to entertain their customers and respond to an ever-changing society.

Consumers seemed to have less free time available for entertainment in the 1990s, so the industry responded with a new concept: the family entertainment center. Unlike larger parks, which required one or two days to fully enjoy, family entertainment centers emphasized activities that could be enjoyed in a short amount of time. Most cities now feature one or more of these facilities, which can range from a large games arcade to a miniature amusement park complete with go-carts and kiddie rides.

Although the industry is increasingly dominated by major corporations and large, high-tech thrill rides, there is a renewed sense of appreciation for the industry's heritage. Two amusement parks—Pittsburgh's Kennywood and Playland in New York—are now listed as National Historic Landmarks, as are numerous rides throughout the country, such as

Cedar Point, in Sandusky, Ohio, is one traditional amusement park that has thrived in the theme park era.

Leap the Dips at Lakemont Park in Altoona, Pennsylvania, saved through grassroots preservation efforts. A few parks, such as Conneaut Lake Community Park in Pennsylvania, have found new life as nonprofit community assets. The few remaining family-owned parks have found ways to peacefully coexist with their large, corporate-owned competitors. Few regions of the country better reflect the industry today than Pennsylvania. Of the thirteen major parks, two are owned by major corporations, two are owned by a nonprofit foundation, one is a nonprofit community asset, and the remainder are family-owned.

As the amusement park industry enters the twenty-first century, it is enjoying unprecedented popularity. In all corners of the world, people flock to their local parks, and thanks to advances in technology, they are thrilled in ways never before imagined. In the United States, over 300 million people visit amusement parks annually—more than twice the number in 1970, despite the fact that the number of parks has remained consistent at around six hundred. The industry seems to have entered a new golden age.

A History of the Amusement Park in Pennsylvania

PENNSYLVANIA IS ONE OF THE COUNTRY'S GREAT AMUSEMENT PARK meccas. Since the industry began in the nineteenth century, nearly four hundred amusement parks have operated in the state, more than in any other, and from the first decade of the twentieth century until the 1960s, Pennsylvania had more operating parks than any other state. This is due to a combination of factors. The rolling terrain separated many small cities and towns, prompting each community to support its own home-town park. The state is an industrial capital with a wealth of coal mines, steel mills, machine shops, and other factories that provided a steady supply of patrons to support the crucial picnic business. In addition, Pennsylvania has a diversity of ethnic groups, many of which brought their heritage of fairs and festivals from their homeland to gathering places throughout the state.

Roots of the Industry

In 1812, Philadelphia became the site of America's first municipal park when 5 acres on the banks of Schuylkill River were landscaped and opened to the public. The park was joined in 1835 by Lemon Hill, a beer garden and recreation area overlooking the river that lasted until the 1880s. Soon recreation areas surrounded the city. Forest Park, which later became a successful amusement park, first hosted picnickers in Chalfont in 1835; Smith's Island, in the Delaware River, acquired a reputation as a place where "anything goes" when it opened in the 1860s;

and the land that later became Hazle Park in the Pocono region started hosting picnics, church outings, and ethnic groups in 1861. One of the Philadelphia area's most enduring amusement parks opened in 1868 when Civil War veteran Hesekiah Zieber opened his farm to picnickers, offering attractions such as boating, palm reading, and monkeys. It later became West Point Park, which lasted until 1989.

And early expansion was not limited to the Philadelphia area. Williams Grove, still operating as an amusement park near Harrisburg, first opened to picnickers in 1850. Pittsburgh-area residents traveled to Ross Grove, starting in the 1850s. By the 1870s, the sites of many of Pennsylvania's current amusement parks, including Conneaut Lake Community Park, Dorney Park, Kennywood, and Lakemont Park, were becoming popular picnic destinations, long before officially opening. These early picnic groves resembled today's municipal parks more than amusement parks. Rides, if there were any, were limited to boats and merry-go-rounds.

Perhaps the greatest of Pennsylvania's early amusements was the Mauch Chunk Switchback Railroad, considered a forerunner of the modern roller coaster. The railroad got its start in 1827, serving coal mines outside what is now the town of Jim Thorpe. Unlike today's railroads, the Switchback Railroad took advantage of the region's mountainous terrain and used gravity to carry coal on an 18-mile round-trip between the towns of Mauch Chunk and Summit Hill. The route started in Mauch Chunk at the base of Mount Pisgah, where donkeys and, later, special

The 18-mile-long Mauch Chunk Switchback Railroad started with this climb up the 662-foot-tall Mount Pisgah. AUTHOR'S COLLECTION

engines hauled the trains to the top of the 662-foot mountain. The train coasted by gravity to the outside of Summit Hill, nearly 9 miles away, where it was hauled 462 feet up Mount Jefferson to the town. The train turned around at Summit Hill and coasted all the way back to Mauch Chunk under gravity power. It was an engineering marvel. By 1872, however, advances in technology had made the railroad obsolete for hauling coal, and it was converted into a tourist attraction. In an age when the primary mode of transportation was horse and buggy, coasting through the mountains at speeds up to 65 miles per hour was a tremendous thrill. Excursion trains from New York and Philadelphia swarmed to Mauch Chunk. In its heyday, only Niagara Falls attracted more tourists. The railway remained a popular attraction until it shut down in 1933, at the height of the Depression.

Trolley Parks

While amusement parks were starting to catch on in the 1870s and 1880s, growth really took off with the advent of trolleys in Pennsylvania. By 1890, the state's first trolley lines were in operation, and soon hundreds of lines opened throughout the state. As in other states, the trolley companies developed amusement parks as a way to increase otherwise slow evening and weekend traffic. Without a string of beaches like New York and New Jersey had to help promote the growth of amusement parks, the impact of the trolley companies in developing the industry in Pennsylvania was especially profound, and five of the twelve trolley parks still in operation in the country are located in this state.

Over the next twenty years, trolley parks opened rapidly in Pennsylvania. Between 1899 and 1905, the number of parks in the state listed by *Billboard* magazine increased from thirty-three to seventy-three. Among the parks opening in the Philadelphia area during the late 1800s and early 1900s were Lenape Park in West Chester, which had been a popular picnic grove since 1877, in 1892; Menlo Park in Perkasie and Carsonia Park in Reading in 1896; and Woodside Park in Philadelphia in 1897.

The northeastern portion of the state saw the opening of Traction Park (later known as Hanson's) in 1891; Rittersville Park (later Central Park) in Allentown and Hazle Park in West Hazleton in 1892; Island Park in Easton in 1894; and Sans Souci Park in Wilkes-Barre and the still operating Bushkill Park, both in 1902. Central Pennsylvania saw the debut of Harrisburg's Paxtang Park in 1893 and Altoona's Lakemont Park, which still survives, in 1894. Among the trolley parks opening in northwest Pennsylvania were Waldameer Park in Erie in 1896. In 1897, the New Castle Traction Company converted the five-year-old Brinton Park into Cascade Park, and Monarch Park in Oil City opened in 1900.

Harrisburg's Paxtang Park was one of the many trolley parks to open in the late 1800s. AUTHOR'S COLLECTION

But probably in no other region of the state was the impact of the trolley park more profound than in the Pittsburgh area. One of the first trolley parks was the short-lived Wilson's Grove, which opened in the town of Washington in 1891. Soon it was joined by Southern Park in Pittsburgh's Carrick section in 1893; Calhoun Park in Pittsburgh in 1895; Oakwood Park in the Pittsburgh suburb of Crafton in 1896; and Pittsburgh's now legendary Kennywood in 1898. Growth continued into the twentieth century, with Oakford Park in Greensburg and Olympia Park in McKeesport opening in 1901; Alameda Park in Butler in 1903; and Lenape Park in Kittanning in 1905.

Growth of the trolley parks soon leveled off, however, and trolley companies began losing interest in the amusement park business. In one of the earliest divestitures, the Pittsburgh Railways Company sold its four parks in Pittsburgh—Kennywood, Southern Park, Oakwood Park, and Calhoun Park—to an investor group, which immediately closed Calhoun and Oakwood. They continued to operate Southern Park until 1910, when they closed it to concentrate on building Kennywood into one of America's best amusement parks.

With waning interest in trolley parks and the simple fact that there were not too many other places to build amusement parks, the number of amusement parks in Pennsylvania remained constant at around seventy up until the Depression.

But trolley companies were not solely responsible for the spread of amusement parks throughout the state. In Philadelphia, entrepreneurs opened Willow Grove in 1896, which soon became renowned for its concerts by John Phillip Sousa. Nearby, Chestnut Hill Park (also known as White City) opened in 1898. The park was never popular with the residents of the affluent neighborhood that surrounded it, and in 1912, three of them bought the park and shut it down.

The spread of the elaborate exposition parks started by Coney Island's Luna Park in New York also found its way to Pennsylvania. Most significant was the opening of Luna Park in Pittsburgh. Constructed in 1905 by Frederick Ingersoll, who was already a well-known builder of roller coasters, Luna Park was located in the urban heart of Pittsburgh and featured a series of elaborate buildings surrounding the park's premier attraction, a large water chute ride. Luna Park featured an extensive live-entertainment lineup, including concert bands and acrobatic, equestrian, aerial, and animal acts. Adorning everything were sixty-seven thousand electric lights.

Ingersoll built similar facilities in Cleveland in 1905 and Scranton, Pennsylvania, Washington, D.C., and Mexico City in 1906, creating the first true chain of amusement parks. He was also operating parks or rides in forty-two cities around the country. Unfortunately, Ingersoll's complex parks, packed into confined urban locations, required almost

Frederick Ingersoll's Luna Park in Pittsburgh was the first park in his Luna Park chain.
AUTHOR'S COLLECTION

constant upgrades, and by 1908, Ingersoll was bankrupt. His Pittsburgh park closed in 1909, Mexico City soon after, Scranton in 1916, and the Washington park a few years later. The Cleveland park held on until 1929. But Ingersoll's legacy was not forgotten. When he died in 1929, he was eulogized as "the tree from which the amusement limbs branched forth."

A Manufacturing Hub

With the American amusement park industry undergoing its greatest period of growth in the early twentieth century, an industry also developed to provide rides to the parks. Pennsylvania, with its strong industrial base and central location in the northeastern part of the United States, soon became a hub for these manufacturers.

Gustav Dentzel was probably the earliest amusement ride manufacturer to set up shop in Pennsylvania. A German cabinetmaker, Dentzel came to America in 1864. In 1867, he started a carousel company, touring with a ride made by his family in Germany. By 1870, he was making carousels for the fledgling American amusement park industry, and by the turn of the century, his factory was known as one of the finest manufacturers of carousels in the country. Dentzel's animals were characterized by their realistic carvings and natural poses. This style soon became known as the Philadelphia style of carousel carving and was embraced by Philadelphia's two other great carousel manufacturers: D. C. Muller & Brother and the Philadelphia Toboggan Company. On Gustav Dentzel's death in 1909, his son William took over and operated the company until his death in 1928, at which time it was liquidated.

D. C. Muller & Brother was founded in 1903 by two former Dentzel employees, Daniel and Alfred Muller. The company manufactured complete carousels and also carved animals for other manufacturers. The Mullers built twelve carousels before closing during World War I. At that point, the brothers returned to the Dentzel factory.

The Philadelphia Toboggan Company, now known as Philadelphia Toboggan Coasters, is probably the greatest and most enduring amusement ride manufacturer in history. The company's roots extend back to 1894, when Edward Joy Morris patented a design for a roller coaster that resembled a large figure eight. The ride featured easy construction, high capacity, and thrills, and it was immediately in demand by amusement parks coast to coast. Hundreds ended up being constructed by Morris and a slew of imitators.

Morris's inventive ways continued in 1896, when he patented a design for a new water ride and incorporated the Morris Chute Company. In 1899, he built his first carousel, for Chestnut Hill Park in Philadelphia,

 **Unique and Historic Attractions**

Auto Race, Kennywood
A forerunner of today's go-cart rides, the Auto Race features a series of small electrically powered cars that zip along a winding wooden track.

Barl of Fun, Bushkill Park
One of the last old-style amusement park fun houses in the country, Barl of Fun still features a rotating barrel and hardwood slide.

Caterpillar, Idlewild and Soak Zone
Forerunner of today's high-speed Himalaya ride, Idlewild's Caterpillar still features the canvas covering that envelops the cars during the ride.

**Dizzy Lizzy's Four Quarters Saloon, Idlewild Park,
and Dutch Wonder House, Dutch Wonderland**
Both of these attractions are modern adaptations of the turn-of-the-century Haunted Swing ride. Hold on tight!

**Flying Scooter, Conneaut Lake Park,
and Flyer, Knoebels Amusement Resort**
A do-it-yourself ride in which you control your car via a large wing mounted in the front. Another rare vintage attraction.

Grand Carousel, Knoebels Amusement Resort
One of the largest and most elaborate carousels still in operation, and one of the last on which you can still catch the brass ring.

Kangaroo, Kennywood
The last Flying Coaster operating at an amusement park. This circular ride consists of a series of cars that jump over a ramp, sending riders flying.

Leap the Dips, Lakemont Park
This is the last remaining figure-eight-style roller coaster, which at one time were located in nearly every amusement park. Built in 1902, this is also the oldest operating roller coaster in the world.

Mister Rogers' Neighborhood, Idlewild and Soak Zone
A trolley ride through the woods, where riders visit with the characters from the Mister Rogers television show. A must-see for fans of the program.

Noah's Ark, Kennywood
Walk-through attraction dating to 1936. Last attraction of its type in the country.

Old Mill, Kennywood
Last water-based dark ride in Pennsylvania. Dating back to 1901, the ride is one of the oldest continuously operating rides in the world.

(continued on page 30)

Unique and Historic Attractions
(continued from page 29)

**Tumble Bug, Conneaut Lake Park,
and Turtle, Kennywood**
Once a midway staple, only a few of these rides remain. Consists of a series of large, circular tubs traveling along an undulating track.

Venetian Swings, Bucktail Camping Resort
A simple rider-powered swing ride once found in almost every amusement park. This is one of the last ones in the country.

**The Whip, Bushkill Park, Dorney Park, Hersheypark,
Idlewild and Soak Zone, Kennywood, and Knoebels Amusement Resort**
The whip, one of the first high-speed circular rides, was invented in 1914, and no state has more in operation than Pennsylvania. When Hersheypark installed its whip in 1995, it was the first new one manufactured in decades.

Zephyr Train, Dorney Park
Built in 1935, this is one of the oldest continuously operating train rides in any amusement park. It features a unique electric drive system.

where a figure eight he had built opened the year before. Soon he had constructed rides for twenty parks throughout the country, and his company had branch offices in Leavenworth, Kansas; Des Moines, Iowa; and Queens, New York.

Morris's success caught the attention of Henry Auchy and Chester Albright, who purchased his company in 1903 and used it as the basis for a new company, the Philadelphia Carousel Company, which was renamed the Philadelphia Toboggan Company (PTC) the next year, when production began.

In its heyday, PTC manufactured almost anything an amusement park would need—water rides, dark rides, fun houses, ballrooms, and buildings—but it achieved its greatest fame for its carousels and roller coasters. The company was known for its large, elaborate carousels, including some of the largest ever made, featuring five rows of horses. Between 1904 and 1934, when the Depression shut down production, PTC built seventy-four carousels, twenty-nine of which remain in operation today.

In 1904, PTC began building roller coasters, and by the late 1920s was selling between 8 and 11 wooden roller coasters annually, building a total of 147, 30 of which remain in operation. The roller coaster division survived the Depression and built some notable rides in the late 1940s. But with large, traditional parks in decline in the years following

World War II, the demand for most of the old-style rides dried up, and PTC survived by selling Skee Ball games, along with the occasional roller coaster. The company built its last roller coaster in 1976, and today it manufactures wooden roller coaster trains.

In addition to the chain of Luna Parks, Frederick Ingersoll also found fame building roller coasters. Seeing the rapid growth of the industry, he formed Ingersoll Construction Company in Pittsburgh in 1901 to supply roller coasters and other rides to amusement parks around the country. He even built entire amusement parks for investors. His most popular product was a figure-eight roller coaster. After building his first one at Kennywood in 1902, business took off, and by 1905, thirty-three of them were in operation.

Competing with Ingersoll in the roller coaster business was T. M. Harton, also of Pittsburgh. Harton got his start at the Chicago World's Fair in 1893 before deciding to open roller coasters and carousels on a concession basis at parks throughout North America. He built nineteen roller coasters before his death in 1919, which signaled the end of the T. M. Harton Company. But two of his employees, Erwin and Edward Vettel, set out on their own to build roller coasters, two of which, at Pennsylvania's Conneaut Lake Community Park and Denver's Lakeside Park, are still in operation.

Pennsylvania manufacturers built other rides as well. In the wake of Pittsburgh resident George Washington Gales Ferris's success with his Ferris wheel at the 1893 World's Columbian Exposition in Chicago, the Philadelphia area's Phoenix Iron and Bridge Company built a 125-foot-tall Ferris wheel for an exposition in Atlanta in 1895. The company became the first manufacturer of Ferris wheels, building several others for amusement parks in Philadelphia; Asbury Park, New Jersey; Coney Island, New York; and Charleston, South Carolina.

Following the initial rush into the industry, the growth of ride manufacturing in Pennsylvania slowed until 1919, when Harry Traver opened Traver Engineering in Beaver Falls, attracted by the town's proximity to Pennsylvania's steel mills. Traver had already established himself in the amusement ride industry, having invented the circle swing ride in 1902. This ride, which Traver thought of while watching seagulls circle a ship's mast during an ocean voyage, was a staple at every amusement park. At his factory, he developed a complete line of rides, also including Tumble Bugs, dark rides, and roller coasters. His timing was fortuitous, as the industry was entering its golden age, and demand was skyrocketing. Traver built hundreds of rides during the 1920s, becoming one of the first large-scale ride producers. But the Depression sent the company into receivership, and in 1932, Traver's plant manager took over the factory, renaming it the R. E. Chambers Company, which lasted until 1962.

In 1923, Lusse Manufacturing started making bumper cars in Philadelphia. Founded in 1895 as a small machine shop, Lusse manufactured cigar boxes, beer bottle washing machines, and carousel machinery. The company came up with the idea for bumper cars in 1922 and tested the concept at Philadelphia's Woodside Park before selling them nationally. Lusse lasted until the early 1990s.

Good Times and Bad

Following the flurry of development through the first decade of the century, amusement park development in the state was scarce through World War I. In the 1920s, it started anew, offsetting the closing of many smaller trolley parks. Unlike the previous boom, driven by trolley companies seeking to stimulate ridership during slow periods, this boom was driven by entrepreneurs seeking to cash in on the emerging automobile culture. As such, no one could expect to open an amusement park without ample parking facilities.

With swimming enjoying newfound popularity in the 1920s, many of these new parks were centered around large swimming pools, including Ideal Park in Johnstown (1921), Rainbow Gardens in McKeesport (1924), and Altoona's Ivyside Park (1925), which likely had one of the largest swimming pools ever constructed—620 feet long by 185 feet wide. Other

Altoona's Ivyside Park featured one of the largest swimming pools ever constructed, at 620 feet by 185 feet. AUTHOR'S COLLECTION

parks opening during this period included Burke's Glen near Pittsburgh and Knoebels Groves in Elysburg in 1926; Harmarville Park near Pittsburgh and Evergreen Park in North St. Johns in 1927; and Willow Mill Park near Harrisburg and Ontelaunee and Indian Trail Parks near Allentown in 1929.

But with the onset of the Depression, Pennsylvania was affected like the rest of the country. Opening new parks was out of the question, and over one-third of the state's parks closed. Spring flooding in 1936 inundated many parks, causing still others, such as Bernesco Park in Nescopeck, already struggling, to shut down. Lakemont Park in Altoona was spared a similar fate when the citizens of Blair Country banded together to save the park.

Given the industrial base of Pennsylvania, many parks enjoyed a renewed prosperity during World War II, as factories throughout the state were running at full capacity. Others, however, such as Croops Glen in Hunlock Creek, Valley View Park in Inkerman, and Olympia Park in McKeesport, closed because of material shortages and access problems in the face of gasoline rationing and never reopened.

As was common in much of the country during this time, Pennsylvania's amusement parks were largely segregated. In 1945, a group of African-American churches in the Pittsburgh area opened Fairview Park to host picnics for groups not welcome at other parks. The park featured a wooden roller coaster and remains open today as a picnic park for everyone, although the rides were removed in 1980.

The fifties were a decade of ups and downs for the state's amusement park industry. Many parks that had been fading since the Depression, such as Junction Park in Beaver Falls and Rock Point Park in Ellwood City, quietly shut their doors. Allentown's Central Park closed in 1951 after the last of a long series of fires destroyed its roller coaster; Hazle Park closed after the 1955 season, as its patrons turned elsewhere for entertainment; and rising property values led to the closure of Philadelphia's Woodside Park in 1956.

But while some parks were closing, the postwar baby boom prompted the opening of several new ones catering to the kid's market. White Swan Park opened in Pittsburgh in 1955, followed in 1957 by Angela Park in Drums and Fantasyland in Gettysburg, one of the state's first theme parks. But the state avoided large-scale kiddieland development, as was common elsewhere in the country, and existing parks soon added large kiddielands of their own.

The situation remained the same through the 1960s. While business at most parks was steady, some parks closed, such as Edgewood Park in Shamokin in 1964 and Willow Park in Bethlehem in 1969. But newer

Willow Grove Park, outside Philadelphia, was one of Pennsylvania's greatest amusement parks but closed in 1975. AUTHOR'S COLLECTION

facilities opened, such as Lancaster's Dutch Wonderland in 1963. The 1960s also marked the end of an era, as trolley service to Pittsburgh's West View Park, the last amusement park in the state to be served by trolleys, ended in 1965.

While the number of amusement parks operating in the state had rebounded since the Depression from forty-five to around sixty, many faced increasing challenges during the 1970s, including slowing population growth, aging facilities, factory closings, and interstate highways facilitating access to larger amusement parks. Robert Ott, formerly of Dorney Park, also observed that many parks relied on roller rinks as a major source of income and were hurt when the popularity of roller skating declined.

Hurricane Agnes inundated the state in June 1972, and the creeks that many parks were built around flooded. Several parks, especially in the central part of the state, were hit hard, including Knoebels Grove in Elysburg; Willow Mill near Harrisburg, whose carousel was almost destroyed when its building collapsed; Hersheypark, which lost its classic mill chute ride; Williams Grove, near Harrisburg, which was almost completely wiped out; and Kishacoquillas Park in Lewistown, which never reopened and whose parts were sold to many other damaged parks to help them rebuild.

After surviving the tumult of the previous three decades, many parks in the larger cities could hold on no longer. The largest park to close during the decade was the once great Willow Grove Park, in the Philadelphia suburbs. After opening in 1896, Willow Grove became known for its band concerts and, according to Robert Ott, was "the Disneyland of its time." But in the 1950s and 1960s, the park, despite its abundance of rides, went into a decline. In a last-ditch attempt to salvage the operation, National Service Industries leased the park in 1971 and attempted to capitalize on the popularity of theme parks by converting it into Six Gun Territory, building a Wild West street, adding a dolphin show, and giving the rides a western flavor. But the public did not respond to the changes, and the park closed in 1975. In September 1980, the abandoned remains of the park were demolished for a shopping mall.

West View Park, outside Pittsburgh, closed its gates for the last time in 1977. Opened in 1906 by the great roller coaster builder T. M. Harton, West View had grown into one of the country's largest amusement parks by the 1960s. But in the wake of a fire that destroyed its ballroom in 1973, a declining population base, and increasingly aggressive competition from nearby Kennywood, West View could no longer hold on. West View sat abandoned until 1980, when it, like Willow Grove, was leveled for a shopping center.

West View Park, near Pittsburgh, one of the country's largest amusement parks, succumbed in 1977. AUTHOR'S COLLECTION

Smaller parks were also struggling. Fun City in Johnstown removed its rides in 1973 to focus on its pool. Indian Trail Park sold off many of its rides and tore down its roller coaster in 1976, but continued to operate. Some parks, to raise capital, sold off their priceless antique carousels, including Lenape Park near Philadelphia in 1978; Ghost Town in the Glen near Scranton, and West Point Park near Philadelphia, both in 1979; and Pine Grove Park north of Harrisburg in 1980. Not surprisingly, these parks closed within a few years.

While these parks were closing, the theme park boom largely avoided the state. Hersheypark transformed itself by adding several themed areas, but the only real attempt to capitalize on this boom was the opening of Magic Valley in the Poconos in 1977. The park, much smaller than the huge corporate theme parks, was built around a turn-of-the-century themed village, complete with Keystone Kops and craftsmen. But with only nine rides, the park could never attract sufficient traffic, and it quietly closed in 1986. The site is now the Pike County fairground.

The summer of 1979 was disastrous for the amusement industry. The weather stunk, gasoline was rationed, and the Three Mile Island nuclear power plant incident outside Harrisburg and a rumored polio outbreak among the Amish diminished tourist traffic. By late July, attendance at some parks was down as much as 33 percent over the previous year.

Probably the industry's most tragic story that season was that of Rocky Springs Park. Rocky Springs had initially closed in 1966, after seventy-nine years of operation. Rather than redevelop the site, the family that owned the land boarded up the park and let it sit there, essentially becoming an amusement park time capsule. In 1978, a group of local businessmen purchased the park and spent $1 million to restore the vintage rides and buildings, creating a living amusement park museum. They also intended to restore the park's legendary roller coaster, the Wildcat, and add newer rides, such as a log flume. This could not have been done at a worse time. Just as the park was struggling to establish itself, traffic evaporated. Rocky Springs soon went into receivership and limped along until 1983, when it closed forever. In 1984, the remains were sold off in a three-day auction, and soon condominiums graced the property.

The challenges of 1979 were just a prelude to what was likely the worst decade in the history of the Pennsylvania amusement park industry. At this point, there were only about three dozen amusement parks operating in the state, 40 percent less than the number three decades earlier. Many of those were limping along, after surviving the 1970s. But soon the state's industrial base went into a deep tailspin. Through the decade, steel mills, coal mines, and factories shut down, and nearly one-fourth of the manufacturing jobs in Pennsylvania were lost. Since many

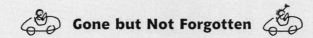 **Gone but Not Forgotten**

More amusement parks have operated in Pennsylvania than in any other state. While Pennsylvania is still blessed with a wealth of parks, all too many are now memories. Here are some of the better-known amusement parks to have operated in the state.

Aliquippa Park, Aliquippa, 1905 to 1908.
Angela Park, Drums, 1957 to 1988.
Brinton Park/Cascade Park, New Castle, 1892 to 1983.
Calhoun Park, Pittsburgh, 1895 to 1906.
Carsonia Park, Reading, 1896 to 1950.
Central Park, Allentown, 1892 to 1951.
Croop's Glen, Hunlock Creek, 1904 to 1941.
Doodlebug Park, Trevorton, 1960s to 1976.
Edgewood Park, Shamokin, early 1900s to 1964.
Fairview Park, Delmont, 1945 to 1980.
Fantasyland, Gettysburg, 1957 to 1980.
Forest Park, Hanover, 1885 to 1967.
Hanover Park/Sans Souci Park, Wilkes-Barre, 1902 to 1970.
Hazle Park, West Hazleton, 1892 to 1956.
Ideal Park and Fun City, Johnstown, 1921 to 1973.
Indian Trail Park, Cherryville, 1929 to 1983.
Island Park, Easton, 1894 to 1919.
Ivyside Park, Altoona, 1925 to 1947.
Kishacoquillas Park, Lewistown, 1920s to 1972.
Lake Ariel Park, Lake Ariel, 1928 to 1955.
Lakeview Park, Royersford, 1940s to 1988.
Lakewood Park, Mahanoy City, 1916 to 1982.
Lenape Park, Kittanning, 1905 to 1928.
Lenape Park/Mainline Park, West Chester, 1890 to 1985.
Luna Park, Pittsburgh, 1905 to 1909.
Luna Park/Island Park, Johnstown, 1904 to 1922.
Magic Valley Village, Bushkill, 1977 to 1986.
Maple View Park, Canonsburg, 1928 to 1930.
Marty's Circus of Fun, Bensalem, 1979 to 1995.
Nay Aug Park, Scranton, 1918 to 1988.
Newton Lake Park, Greenfield Township, 1917 to 1977.
Northern Electric Park, Clarks Summit, 1910 to 1925.
Oakford Park, Jeannette, 1901 to 1938.
Oakwood Park, Crafton, 1896 to 1906.

(continued on page 38)

Gone but Not Forgotten
(continued from page 37)

Old MacDonalds Farm, Butler, 1961 to 1970s.
Olympia Park, McKeesport, 1901 to 1942.
Ontelaunee Park, New Tripoli, 1929 to 1988.
Paxtang Park, Harrisburg, 1893 to 1929.
Rainbow Gardens, White Oak, 1924 to 1968.
Rocky Glen Park, Moosic, 1904 to 1987.
Rocky Springs Park, Lancaster, 1887 to 1983.
Rolling Green Park, Sunbury, 1912 to 1971.
Shady Grove Park, Uniontown, 1885 to 1974.
Traction Park/Hanson's Amusement Park, Harveys Lake, 1891 to 1984.
Valley View Park, Inkerman, 1904 to 1941.
West View Park, Pittsburgh, 1906 to 1977.
White Swan Park, Coraopolis, 1955 to 1989.
Willow Amusement Park, Butztown, 1929 to 1969.
Willow Grove Park/Six Gun Territory, Willow Grove, 1896 to 1975.
Willow Mill Park, Mechanicsburg, 1929 to 1989.
Woodside Park, Philadelphia, 1897 to 1956.
Zieber's Park/West Point Park, West Point, 1868 to 1988.

of the parks relied on industrial picnics for a majority of their business, this loss was just too much.

Other factors made it tough for many smaller parks to survive. In 1984, in the wake of a series of amusement park accidents outside the state, the Amusement Inspection Act was signed into law in Pennsylvania, requiring every park to have its rides inspected monthly and to carry $1 million in insurance. As a result, many parks saw their insurance rates increase up to 300 percent.

The result of all this was that park closings became an all-too-common occurrence during the 1980s. In 1980, the owner of Fantasyland retired, selling the land to the government and the rides to a theme park developer in Ohio. Lakewood Park in Mahanoy City closed in 1982 after sixty-six years of operation, following a long decline. Cascade Park in New Castle and Indian Trail Park near Allentown both shut down in 1983 in the face of dwindling business and deteriorating facilities. Hanson's Amusement Park in Harveys Lake closed in 1984 because of the increasing insurance premiums, although the park had already declined to the point where it had not had the funds to fix its roller coaster after it broke down in 1980. Lenape Park, outside Philadelphia, gave its final rides in 1985, after ninety-five years of operation, and Trout Pond Park near Williamsport removed its rides that year, as the park could no longer afford to maintain them.

Another park that had been in a long-term decline, Altoona's Lakemont Park, was converted in 1986 into a theme park operated by the Boyer Brothers Candy Company. Known as Boyertown, it opened over-budget and overpriced and was a miserable failure. The park struggled to survive for several years in the face of bankruptcy and limited finances, but it managed to turn around and remained open.

In 1987, Rocky Glen, outside Scranton, also succumbed after a decades-long struggle with the decline of the coal industry in that region. In the early 1970s, it had been converted to a theme park, Ghost Town in the Glen, but it soon went back to its original name and did away with the Wild West theme. In 1988, the Hare Krishnas attempted to purchase the park for a temple, but the idea was quickly dropped in the face of local opposition. Lakeview Park in Royersford, outside Philadelphia, also opened for the last time in 1987.

By 1988, the situation had become dire. An article in the Philadelphia *Inquirer,* on the declining number of amusement parks in the eastern part of the state detailed many of the causes, including runaway insurance costs, a dwindling labor pool, aggressive competition, and the rising costs of new rides.

The sad decline of Rocky Glen Park, Moosic, epitomized the plight of the industry in the 1980s.

That year, Angela Park in Drums was foreclosed upon in the face of skyrocketing insurance costs. West Point Park, near Philadelphia, also closed in 1988 after 120 years, as it could not afford to comply with new local regulations requiring the park to tie in with local sewer lines. In 1989, Willow Mill Park, outside Harrisburg, couldn't make it through the season, due to increased insurance costs and declining attendance, closing on June 30, after sixty years.

When the 1980s ended, seventeen amusement parks had closed throughout the state, nearly half the number that had been in operation at the beginning of the decade.

But all was not bleak. Sesame Place opened in 1981 outside Philadelphia, introducing a new concept in amusement parks to the country. Kennywood, near Pittsburgh, continued to expand in the face of a depressed local economy and was named a National Historic Landmark in 1987. Dorney Park in Allentown bounced back from a disastrous fire in 1984 and launched a major expansion that continues to this day. Knoebels Amusement Resort in Elysburg put itself on the map by successfully moving a wooden roller coaster from Texas and reopening it. Though the previous two decades had taken a horrible toll on the Pennsylvania amusement park industry, there was still hope.

A New Golden Age

In October 1990, an auction was held at White Swan Park just outside Pittsburgh. The thirty-five-year-old park stood in the path of a new expressway and was forced to close after the 1989 season, the eighteenth closure in ten years. But just a few miles away, at Kennywood, construction was under way on the Steel Phantom, the world's tallest and fastest roller coaster, an event that again focused the attention of the world on Pennsylvania. This marked a turning point. Recovery had now begun, and the Pennsylvania amusement park industry was entering a new golden age. Throughout the next decade, the surviving parks emerged stronger than ever and were poised to benefit as Pennsylvania's economy slowly improved.

One of the first tentative signs that the industry in Pennsylvania was bouncing back occurred in Jim Thorpe, home of the long-gone Mauch Chunk Switchback Railway. In 1986, a group had formed with the intent of rebuilding the railroad, and in 1991, they opened a 150-foot-long replica of the line to generate interest in rebuilding the remainder of the railroad to once again entertain thrill seekers. Plans continue today.

Many of the parks that had survived were now in a better position than ever to take advantage of improved economic conditions. Waldameer Park in Erie undertook a major expansion that saw the addition of one of the state's largest water parks. DelGrosso's Amusement Park in Tipton awoke from a decades-long slumber to add new rides and a water park. Lakemont Park spent most of the decade rebounding from its disastrous Boyertown experiment and in 1999 was able to restore Leap the Dips, the world's oldest roller coaster, after it had been closed for nearly fifteen years. Bushkill Park was purchased by new owners and restored in 1990.

Pennsylvania even reemerged as a home to manufacturers. Philadelphia Toboggan Coasters was able to ride a revival of roller coaster construction to newfound prosperity and in 1998 announced its intention to again build carousels, with the first one going to the new Please Touch Museum in Philadelphia. A new company, Great Coasters International, set up shop in Sunbury, selling wooden roller coasters based on the twisting creations of the 1920s. Its first ride, the Wildcat, opened in 1996 at Hersheypark, which itself was undergoing renewed expansion in the 1990s.

Not all the news in Pennsylvania was good, however. Conneaut Lake Community Park struggled for much of the decade, trying to find a niche in an increasingly competitive marketplace. Despite all the challenges it faced—aging rides and buildings, bankruptcy, ownership turmoil, and tight finances—the park has survived and is finding new life as a nonprofit community park. Tucked away in remote corners of the state are amusement park graveyards. Pieces of Lake Ariel Park, which closed in 1955, can still be found in the woods near Scranton. The same can be said of Monarch Park, near Oil City, which closed in 1928. Rocky Glen has met a sadder end, slowly being picked apart by arsonists and vandals.

Several other parks, such as Willow Mill Park near Harrisburg, Indian Trail Park near Allentown, and Kishacoquillas Park in Lewistown, remain open as municipal parks, still serving their original role as community gathering places. Ontelaunee Park near Allentown, which has been abandoned since its 1988 closing, might also find new life as a township park. Lenape Park, outside Philadelphia, even more reflects its former life, now operating as Brandywine Picnic Park, a group picnic facility that features a few rides.

At the beginning of the twenty-first century, the parks in Pennsylvania that have survived are enjoying newfound prosperity. They have learned to adapt to changing times, adding new attractions but still respecting their history.

Williams Grove Amusement Park

OPENED 1850

WILLIAMS GROVE AMUSEMENT PARK IS THE ANTITHESIS OF THE MODERN amusement park. It is not adjacent to an interstate highway, and there are no towering rides or flashy signs to tempt passersby, and when you find the place, thick trees hide the amusements from the parking lot. But the search is worth the effort. Williams Grove Amusement Park embodies the spirit of an old-fashioned picnic park with low-key rides, a small lake, a sprawling picnic grove, and a nostalgic midway lined with concessions.

Meeting at the Grove

Back in 1850, the Williams family started hosting picnics on their farm along the banks of Yellow Breeches Creek. As picnics became more popular, people started building cottages for summer stays, and soon a merry-go-round appeared.

In 1872, the Dillsburg & Mechanicsville Railroad was completed, providing easy access to the picnic grove from throughout the region. This easy access prompted the Grangers, a farmers' organization, to hold a one-day Interstate Picnic Exhibition at the park. It was a huge success, and the following year, another railroad, the Cumberland Valley Railroad, leased the park from the Williams family and started developing the grove into a fairground to host the exhibition. By 1874, the exhibition had evolved from a simple social gathering to a trade show, with major farm equipment manufacturers from throughout the country displaying their wares. Soon the fair was expanded to an entire week,

Williams Grove Amusement Park
One Park Ave.
Mechanicsburg, PA 17055
717-697-8266
www.williamsgrovepark.com

Grangers Pic Nic.
Williams Grove, Pa.

Williams Grove came into its own when it became host to the Grangers' Picnic in 1872. COLLECTION OF INGRID HUGHES

and people arrived for extended stays, camping, renting cottages, and staying in hotels.

By 1887, Williams Grove had evolved into a full-blown fairground, with a hotel, two-thousand-seat auditorium, exhibit halls, animal barns, and tent and cottage areas. In addition to the agricultural exhibits, parades and lectures were featured attractions. The fair was at its zenith, with up to thirty-two thousand people arriving daily on one thousand trains.

During World War I, the fair went into a decline. Many of the old buildings were torn down, and in 1918, the Williams family sold the park to Charles Markley. But he was not able to revive the operation, and in 1924, the Richwine family purchased the old fairgrounds.

With amusement parks enjoying tremendous popularity, the Richwines were intent on reviving the picnic grove by converting it into a full-blown amusement park, despite the fact that railroad service to the park had all but ceased.

The Amusement Park Era

By 1928, rides began appearing, including a used carousel that still operates, a Caterpillar, a whip, and a Ferris wheel. The park undertook a major expansion in 1929 by adding a bumper car ride, a Tilt-A-Whirl, and the Swooper, a ride that resembled an oblong Ferris wheel. Also

 VISITING

WILLIAMS GROVE AMUSEMENT PARK

LOCATION

Williams Grove Park is located southwest of Harrisburg, just off U.S. Route 15, about 3 miles south of Exit 236 of the Pennsylvania Turnpike.

OPERATING SCHEDULE

Williams Grove Park is open from Memorial Day to Labor Day, but is closed Mondays, except holidays. Gates open at 10 A.M., the water slides open at 10:30 A.M., and the rides open at 11 A.M. Closing time is 6 P.M. during the week and 8 P.M. on weekends.

ADMISSION

You can pay a one-price admission for under $20 that covers all rides and the water slides, or purchase a general admission for under $5 and then buy individual ride tickets as desired. The go-carts, games, and miniature golf are paid for separately. Parking is free.

FOOD

Williams Grove has several food stands offering a variety of foods, such as pizza, chicken nuggets, hot dogs, and ice cream. You may bring your own food into the park. Tables are available on a first-come, first-served basis.

FOR CHILDREN

Most of Williams Grove's nine kiddie rides are located along the lakefront, including a kiddie roller coaster and a miniature truck ride. Several rides at Williams Grove Park can be enjoyed by the entire family, including the train and carousel.

SPECIAL FEATURES

The Cyclone roller coaster is the last remaining roller coaster built by Oscar Bitler, who built dozens of rides in Pennsylvania and New York in the 1920s and 1930s.

The Williams Grove Historical Steam Engine Association operates a full-size steam train through the fairgrounds. It runs on a 3-mile track during the fair and other special events.

TIME REQUIRED

The park can be enjoyed in as little as four hours.

TOURING TIPS

The park offers a discounted ride and slide pass in the evenings and on weekdays.

Check the schedule of the adjacent Williams Grove Speedway (www.williams grove.com), and combine a car race with your visit to the park. Races are held every Friday and occasional Sundays.

constructed was a dance hall, now used as a theater. These changes allowed Williams Grove Park to thrive even as the Depression closed hundreds of amusement parks around the country. To attract cost-conscious customers, Williams Grove offered free parking, free admission, and weekly fireworks. By 1933, business was strong enough to add a major new roller coaster.

The new ride, called the Zipper, was built by Oscar Bitler, a leading roller coaster builder of the era, and ran along the banks of the creek. Still in operation, it stands 65 feet tall and has a 60-foot maximum drop and 2,300 feet of track. It is an out-and-back design, with a unique structure in which the return leg travels directly underneath the outbound leg. When it opened, Williams Grove claimed that it was the only new roller coaster built in the country in two years.

The park's train ride, the Out & Back (O&B) Railroad, debuted in 1938, as did the Playhouse theater. The next year, the Richwines launched their biggest expansion, purchasing an adjacent farm and opening the Williams Grove Speedway. Although World War II was raging, Williams Grove was able to expand in 1942, with the addition of the Laff in the Dark dark ride and the Loop-O-Plane. To support the war effort, Williams Grove repainted

During its fairground period, the atmosphere at Williams Grove Park more resembled a small town than an amusement park. COLLECTION OF INGRID HUGHES

The Cyclone, formerly the Zipper, has been thrilling riders at Williams Grove since 1933.

the park in patriotic colors and renamed one of the rides the Victory Ride, with all proceeds going to the war effort. But with rationing in full effect, Williams Grove was forced to close for the 1943 and 1944 seasons.

When the war ended and Williams Grove reopened, things were different. The closure had sent people elsewhere, and nearby Hersheypark had expanded and become a stronger competitor. Although a few kiddie rides and a showboat were added, the park stagnated.

In 1959, however, an organization of local steam enthusiasts seeking a place to display their antique steam equipment approached the Richwines about reviving the Great Grangers' Picnic. As a result, for much of the 1960s, Williams Grove's main attractions were the picnic and the speedway. The Richwines, finding it increasingly difficult to compete, started looking for a buyer for the aging facility.

A Place to Park Some Rides

By the early 1970s, the future of Williams Grove was being determined several hundred miles to the east, at Palisades Amusement Park in New Jersey. At the time, the park was one of the largest in the world, and it was known throughout the country as the place where the latest spectacular European rides would be introduced to American thrill seekers. They were imported into the country by Morgan Hughes, owner of most of the rides at Palisades.

Born in Dublin, Ireland, Hughes had come to the United States in 1950 at age thirty, following a career in the British Army, to deliver a rotor ride to Palisades Park on behalf of a friend. Seeing a potential market, he decided to remain in the country and set up a ride-importing business, purchasing flashy new European rides and setting them up at Palisades Park as a way to introduce them to the American amusement park industry. But while Palisades was arguably one of the most successful amusement parks in the country, its location in a congested residential area overlooking Manhattan meant that the land was quite valuable to developers.

While skiing in Switzerland in late 1971, Hughes received word that Palisades would be closed and redeveloped into apartments, and that he had four months to remove his fifty-six rides from the property. Hughes scrambled to find new homes for the rides, but he also wanted to remain active in the business and needed a place to set up the rides he retained. He had heard that Williams Grove was for sale and immediately agreed to purchase the park, sight unseen, for $1.3 million.

The park that Hughes had agreed to purchase had fallen on hard times. It had only a few old rides, including the carousel, train, dark ride, bumper cars, and roller coaster, which had not run in three years, as a tree had fallen across the structure. According to Hughes, everything in the park, from buildings to benches, had been painted with aluminum paint that the Richwines had obtained inexpensively as surplus from a nearby army depot.

Hughes immediately went to work improving the park. The Zipper was renovated and renamed the Cyclone, and several flashy European rides from Palisades Park were installed, including the Zugspitz, a spinning ride, Grand Prix Skooter, Flight to Mars dark ride, the Giant Wheel, and the Allotria fun house.

The new Williams Grove Park opened in early June 1972, but three weeks later, Hurricane Agnes swept through the area, and the Yellow Breeches Creek overflowed its banks, covering the park with up to 10 feet of water. "There was not a house or building on the property that wasn't affected," says Hughes. Rides were swamped, sixty-five cottages that were scattered throughout the grounds were damaged beyond repair, and semi trailers filled with merchandise were swept down the midway and thrown up against the roller coaster. It was a scene of complete devastation.

But Hughes was undeterred, and despite the fact that the National Guard placed the area under lockdown, a crew of 250 worked to get the park reopened, repairing the rides, cleaning up the buildings, and hauling off debris. Since country concerts were a popular draw for Williams

Grove, putting the Playhouse back in operation was a priority. Hughes had a bulldozer go through the theater to remove the two thousand waterlogged seats. The floor was then blacktopped, and a local lumberyard was pressed into service to build new seats.

Miraculously, the park was ready to open for the Fourth of July. Since most of the other area amusement parks were still closed, Hughes advertised heavily on the radio that Williams Grove would be open. People "came in swarms," Hughes recalls.

Over the next several seasons, the park featured a constantly changing ride lineup, as Hughes imported rides and placed them in operation at Williams Grove until they were sold. A major expansion took place in 1978, with the addition of a showboat ride, water slides, a miniature golf course, and a new miniature train.

In July 1980, a tornado hit the park. Fortunately, no one was injured, as the park had closed for the day thirty minutes earlier, but many rides were damaged. The park again recovered, however.

In 1985, the dark ride was refurbished and renamed Dante's Inferno. The Chair-O-Plane and Music Express rides were added that year, the Tilt-A-Whirl and Tea Cup rides in 1999, and two go-cart tracks, one for kids and one for adults, in 2000. As the new millennium dawned,

The Allotria fun house was one of the rides relocated to Williams Grove when Palisades Park closed in 1971.

Generations have strolled the midway at Williams Grove.

Williams Grove expanded the midway into a new part of the park, with a second roller coaster, the Wildcat, a steel-track ride that is 45 feet tall and 1,509 feet long.

Williams Grove Today

Today Williams Grove Park is a throwback to the tree-shaded picnic parks of yesteryear. It offers a total of twenty-two rides, including nine for kids, water slides, a miniature golf course, and a variety of other attractions. The park is surrounded by Yellow Breeches Creek, has a small lake in the middle, and has two entrances, one at the fairgrounds and one near the Williams Grove Speedway.

Located near the speedway entrance are the Wildcat roller coaster, miniature golf course, water slides, and go-carts. The main midway, which runs from the speedway entrance to the Cyclone roller coaster, is the heart of the park and features most of the food and game concessions, Dante's Inferno dark ride, the train station, and the carousel. Between the main midway and the fairgrounds entrance are the picnic grove, kiddieland, fun house, and gift shop.

Williams Grove features several live shows, including a magic show and karaoke. Special events include Antique Car Day, the Model Car Show, and the Great Grange Fair. Held from the last Sunday in August through Labor Day, the fair features a daily steam engine parade, a historical steam engine exhibit, a flea market, auctions, and nightly country and western entertainment.

Idlewild
and Soak Zone

OPENED 1878

ROUTE 30 EAST OF PITTSBURGH IS A CLASSIC PENNSYLVANIA ROAD. AS IT leaves the shopping centers and car dealers of urbanized Pittsburgh, the road starts snaking though small towns and the heavily wooded valleys of the Laurel Highlands. As you approach Ligonier, a typical small Pennsylvania town with vintage buildings clustered around a town square, you can see picnic pavilions and oversize storybook characters on the south side of the highway through the towering trees. As you venture further into the woods, all of the trappings of a full-blown amusement park come into view—a gigantic playground complete with slides and a pool of colorful balls; a re-created western town; distinctive white-sided, red-roofed concession buildings; a wealth of rides; and even a full-scale water park. You've discovered Idlewild Park, considered by many the most beautiful amusement park in the country.

A Rustic Escape

Idlewild Park owes its existence to the Ligonier Valley Railroad, which was originally chartered in 1853. Construction had not begun on the railroad by 1871, and Judge Thomas Mellon, one of the railroad's creditors, purchased the charter at a sheriff's sale. He began construction of the railroad in July 1877, and by December, the 10-mile stretch from Latrobe to Ligonier was completed to serve the coal mines and lumber camps in the region.

Judge Mellon, an astute businessman, wanted to build passenger traffic to complement the

Idlewild Park
P.O. Box C
Ligonier, PA 15658
724-238-3666
www.idlewild.com

Idlewild's original building, a railroad depot built in 1878, still stands at the park.

freight business on the railroad. An obvious strategy was to develop a pleasure resort along the line, a practice that was just beginning to spread throughout the United States. The logical choice for this resort was Idlewild, the estate of William M. Darlington, a 350-acre tract nestled in a picturesque mountain valley, covered with forests and bisected by the tranquil Loyalhanna Creek.

On May 1, 1878, William Darlington granted "the Ligonier Valley Railroad Company the right and privilege to occupy [the land] for picnic purposes or pleasure grounds . . . without compensation in the shape of rent for three years from the first of April 1878 provided no timber or other trees are to be cut or injured." The stipulation protecting the trees has guided park development to this day.

Construction began immediately, and the first structure built at the new park was the train depot. A modest structure, measuring 10 by 25 feet, the depot was considered the smallest full-service station in the United States. It still stands in the park today.

As the railroad's initial lease with Darlington limited the park to a narrow strip of land between the railroad track and the north bank of the creek, it had become quite crowded by the mid-1880s. As a result, management expanded to the south side of Loyalhanna Creek after the construction of a bridge, which is still in use today. For the next several years, activity was concentrated on this side of the creek, where patrons could go boating in the newly dug Lake Woodland. On the Fourth of July

VISITING

IDLEWILD AND SOAK ZONE

LOCATION

Idlewild Park is located 2 miles west of Ligonier on U.S. Route 30. The park is accessible from Exit 67 or 91 of the Pennsylvania Turnpike (I-76). From Exit 67, take Route 30 East about 26 miles directly to the park. From Exit 91, take PA Route 711 North for 12 miles to Route 30 West, and proceed about 2 miles to Idlewild.

OPERATING SCHEDULE

Idlewild Park opens in mid-May for weekend operation. The park is open daily, except Mondays, from Memorial Day weekend through the end of August and on Labor Day weekend. Park gates open at 10 A.M., and most of the rides and attractions open at 11 A.M.

ADMISSION

Admission is less than $25 per person and entitles guests to all rides and attractions, including the water park and parking. Games and miniature golf are extra. Children two years and under are free, and discounts are available for senior citizens.

FOOD

About twenty-five food locations are scattered throughout the park, ranging from portable carts to a cafeteria-style restaurant. Major facilities include Pasta Works in Olde Idlewild, featuring pizza, pasta, and Italian sausage; Mine Shaft Kitchen in Hootin' Holler, with four stands including the BBQ Pit offering ribs, chicken, smoked turkey legs, and corn on the cob; the Potato Patch, selling Idlewild's famous french fries; and Tidbits, serving wraps, salads, and desserts. Big Eddie's Poolside Grill in the Soak Zone offers hamburgers, and Ricky Raccoon's in Raccoon Lagoon serves burgers, chicken strips, hot dogs, and salads. Throughout the park, you can find tacos, Philly cheese steaks, pizza, ice cream, funnel cakes, and soft pretzels. You may also bring your own food into the park. Parking is available adjacent to the picnic pavilions.

FOR CHILDREN

Although it's fun for everyone, the entire park is geared for children under twelve years of age. Smaller kids will especially enjoy Raccoon Lagoon, Mister Rogers' Neighborhood, Jumpin' Jungle, and Story Book Forest.

Special kids' meals are available at Big Eddie's Poolside Grill, the Mine Shaft BBQ Pit, and Ricky Raccoon's.

SPECIAL FEATURES

Mister Rogers' Neighborhood is Idlewild's signature attraction. Visitors board a replica of the Neighborhood Trolley to travel to the Neighborhood of Make-Believe to visit with all of the residents.

The antique carousel was hand carved by the Philadelphia Toboggan Company and has operated at Idlewild since 1931.

(continued on page 54)

VISITING (continued from page 53)

Story Book Forest is one of the country's last remaining storybook attractions, dozens of which dotted America's roadsides during the 1950s. Idlewild's is the largest one remaining and one of the best preserved.

TIME REQUIRED

Plan on spending an entire day at Idlewild, especially if you visit with kids and plan to enjoy Soak Zone, see the shows, and take advantage of the picnic facilities.

TOURING TIPS

Visit during the week, as crowds tend to be lighter.

Story Book Forest opens at 10 A.M., one hour earlier than the rest of the park. If you arrive before 11 A.M., go there first, and then head straight to Olde Idlewild, as this section tends to be the most crowded later in the day. Also try to hit Mister Rogers' Neighborhood early, as it's the most popular ride in the park and often has the longest lines.

The Loyalhanna train provides convenient transportation between Hootin' Holler and Raccoon Lagoon and Mister Rogers' Neighborhood.

1890, the trains traveling to the park were so crowded that, according to the Ligonier *Echo,* "the tops of the coaches were covered with boys."

In the early 1890s, the park was able to expand on the north side of the creek, where the train depot was located. Many of the structures from the expansion still exist today. Attractions included boating on Lake St. Clair, pavilions for dining and dancing, ballfields, and tennis courts. A merry-go-round first appeared around this time.

The growing crowds at the park prompted an additional expansion for the 1896 season that included the construction of Lake Bouquet, the park's main lake. A new merry-go-round was operated as a concession by the T. M. Harton Company, a major builder and operator of carousels and roller coasters, based in Pittsburgh. Powered by a steam engine, the merry-go-round was placed in a beautiful new pavilion in the center of the park.

By 1898, Idlewild's attractions included a bicycle track around Lake Bouquet, swan boats and boat launches in the lake, and a hiking trail on the island in the center of the lake; fishing in Loyalhanna Creek; and rowboats in Lake St. Clair. Park buildings, many of which are still in use, included a bandstand, boathouse, women's cottage, large dining hall, and pavilion that served as an auditorium and dance hall. Along the banks of Loyalhanna Creek were a smaller dining hall, auditorium, and amphitheater. The rustic area on the south side of the creek, dubbed the Woodlands, offered swings, tables, rustic seating, walks, gardens, and an athletic field.

A Change of Pace

In 1931, the Idlewild Management Company took control of the park. The company consisted of Richard Mellon, son of park founder Thomas Mellon, and Clinton C. Macdonald. Macdonald, who took over the operational responsibilities of the park, brought over thirty-five years of amusement park management experience to Idlewild. Initially, Mellon wanted to develop a major amusement park along the lines of its Pittsburgh competitors, Kennywood and West View Park. Macdonald, however, insisted that they take a slow, steady, low-key approach to park expansion, and he eventually prevailed. "I can build here the rest of my life," his son C.K. (Jack) recalled him saying, and that's exactly what he did.

The park that the Idlewild Management Company took over in 1931 had changed little in thirty years. It had no utilities, and its only rides were a thirty-five-year-old, steam-powered merry-go-round and the old swan boats and rowboats. The only lighting was two emergency lights powered by an old Studebaker engine. What the park did have, however, was its incredible natural beauty and a stop on the Ligonier Valley Railroad.

For the park's 1931 season, the new owners installed a bumper car ride and a swan swing, Idlewild's first kiddie ride. They also replaced the original merry-go-round with a modern, $24,000 Philadelphia Toboggan Company carousel that featured forty-eight hand-carved horses and two chariots. It was the eighty-third carousel manufactured by the company, one of the last made before the Depression shut down

Idlewild's atmosphere was much more sedate in the early 1900s. AUTHOR'S COLLECTION

production. The new ride was placed in the existing carousel building, where it remains to this day. The owners also illuminated the park with over five thousand electric lights and, to enhance the natural beauty of the park, planted ten thousand shrubs.

Although the Depression was causing hundreds of amusement parks around the country to close, Idlewild Park continued to steadily expand throughout the 1930s. In 1932, a swimming pool was added on the island in Lake Bouquet. So that the pool would be ready in time for the park opening, construction proceeded through the winter under huge canvases covering the work area. The 80-by-200-foot pool was a huge success and helped attract a crowd of fifteen thousand on the Fourth of July. The owners also added more rides: a Custer Car ride, a forerunner of today's auto turnpike rides; an airplane circle swing; a Ferris wheel; and a new dark ride—the Rumpus, which unfortunately was destroyed in a fire in 1947.

For the 1938 season, Idlewild added Rollo Coaster, a 27-foot-tall, 900-foot-long wooden roller coaster designed by the Philadelphia Toboggan Company that remains a favorite ride to this day. The wood for the ride was cut from trees harvested on the Idlewild Park property, using a sawmill built next to the construction site. The unique out-and-back ride was constructed on a hillside, with the ride's outbound leg running through the woods along the top of the hill and the inbound leg running along the bottom.

Despite the Depression, Idlewild Park drew steady crowds. AUTHOR'S COLLECTION

Rollo Coaster was built on a hillside in 1938.

The 1939 season marked the debut of the Idlewild Express miniature railroad, manufactured by the Dayton Fun House Corporation and running on a 4,000-foot-long track that completely circled Lake Bouquet. A 70-foot-long tunnel and several thousand evergreen trees planted along the route enhanced the ride. The express ran in the park for fifty-eight years before its retirement in 1997. Their present whip ride was ordered by the Macdonalds during their trip to the Mangels Company factory in Brooklyn, while visiting the New York World's Fair, and it was installed in 1939 as well.

During the 1941–42 off-season, the United States entered World War II. Rationing severely hampered park operation during the 1942 season. By the start of the 1943 season, the Macdonalds decided to close the park, as gas rationing and suspension of service on the railroad made it difficult for people to get to Idlewild. The park remained closed for the duration of the war.

After the war's end in 1945, much work was needed to bring Idlewild back to its owners' high standards. The Macdonalds spent $50,000 in renovations, and Idlewild reopened in May 1946. The 1947 season marked the debut of the Caterpillar, the first new ride added to Idlewild in eight years. Soon the Macdonald family acquired complete control of Idlewild Park, purchasing the land in 1948 and the park itself in 1950.

As the 1950s dawned, the postwar baby boom was in full swing. To take advantage of the ever-increasing numbers of small children, the

Story Book Forest was added as a separate attraction in 1956. AUTHOR'S COLLECTION

Macdonalds spent the decade adding new kiddie attractions. Three kiddie rides were added for the 1950 season, and the following two seasons were spent consolidating all of the kiddie rides along the north bank of Loyalhanna Creek and constructing a completely fenced-in Kiddieland. Additional kiddie rides were added to Kiddieland between 1954 and 1956, including the Hand Cars (1954), the Street Car (1955), a Ferris wheel (1955), and the Turtle (1956), all of which remain in operation.

For a number of years, the Ligonier Valley Railroad had experienced a decline in freight traffic, due to the closing of area coal mines, and in passenger traffic, as a result of the rise of the automobile. In 1952, the railroad shut down, and the atmosphere of Idlewild Park was forever changed. As a testament to the growing influence of the automobile, Idlewild Park converted the former five-track railroad siding that was used to park picnic trains into a parking lot two years later.

While on vacation in New England, the Macdonalds visited a small roadside attraction that featured displays of favorite children's stories and felt that a similar attraction would be the perfect complement to Idlewild. The result was Story Book Forest, which opened in 1956. This children's area was a lively collection of fifteen lifesize displays of famous nursery rhymes, such as the Old Woman in the Shoe, Jack Be Nimble, Humpty Dumpty, and the Crooked Man. The displays were clustered around a pond dug by a local resident using a mule-drawn shovel. Unlike the amusement park, which was located away from the highway, Story

Book Forest took full advantage of the thousands of cars passing by on Route 30, with a fanciful castle entrance along the road. Operated as a separate attraction, Story Book Forest was an immediate success, drawing eighty-four thousand customers from as far away as Ohio and Maryland in its first season.

At the end of the decade, C. C. Macdonald passed away, leaving his two sons, Jack and Richard, to take over the legacy he had created. They continued expansion in the mid-1960s with a zoo called Frontier Safariland and the Loyalhanna Express, a miniature train ride manufactured by Crown Metal Works of Elizabeth, Pennsylvania. The express crossed Loyalhanna Creek, linking Idlewild Park to Story Book Forest and Frontier Safariland.

With the rapid expansion of the theme park industry in the mid-1970s putting the squeeze on many smaller, traditional parks, Idlewild kept up its pace of expansion with new rides and a new thematic attraction, the Historic Village, built for the nation's bicentennial in 1976. Located next to Story Book Forest, the Historic Village was patterned after a small nineteenth-century town, with a general store, the Feed Bin restaurant, a sheriff's office and jail, a blacksmith shop, a woodcraft shop, the Copper Penny Saloon, and the newspaper and lawyer's office, where customers could get souvenir documents printed to order.

Bigger and Better

In 1982, after running the park for more than fifty years, the Macdonalds decided to put the 400-acre facility up for sale. The family initially received an offer from a group that planned to develop Idlewild into a major theme park. Getting wind of this offer, the Kennywood Park Corporation, a friendly rival for many years with its own park, Kennywood, near Pittsburgh, decided to buy the park.

Not wanting to compete with their own successful park down the road, the new owners decided to avoid adding big thrill rides and concentrate on maintaining Idlewild as a park for children, as the Macdonalds had done. "We never wanted to make a big park," Jack Macdonald recalled. "It wasn't a job, it was an avocation." That was a key factor in Idlewild's atmosphere and was something that Kennywood sought to preserve and enhance in its commitment to maintaining the park's natural beauty and family atmosphere.

The first major addition was Jumpin' Jungle, a children's play area constructed in the woods as a link between the amusement area and Story Book Forest. The following year, the Historic Village was relocated from next to Story Book Forest to the park's former maintenance area between Jumpin' Jungle and the original amusement area. Renamed

Hootin' Holler, the buildings from the former village became part of a re-creation of a Wild West town that also featured a shooting gallery, games, live shows, and Confusion Hill—a tour of a gravity-defying tilt house.

Taking advantage of the water park boom that was spreading across the country, Idlewild added the H2Ohhhh Zone, a complex of four water slides located next to the park's swimming pool, in 1985. Three years later, Rafter's Run, a pair of "dry" water slides, was installed. After climbing to the top of a 50-foot tower, two riders sit in a rubber raft and are sent down a 402-foot-long, 42-inch-diameter tube into a splash-down pool.

Another important project that began in 1985 was a two-year restoration of the park's magnificent antique carousel. All of the horses were stripped to bare wood, repaired, and given two coats of paint and two coats of varnish. The carousel's band organ, machinery, murals, and organ facade were also restored.

Idlewild made its largest single investment to date in 1989, with the opening of Mister Rogers' Neighborhood of Make-Believe. Fred Rogers, creator of the famous PBS children's television show, grew up in nearby Latrobe and visited the park often as a child. Impressed with the changes that the Kennywood Park Corporation had made over the last several seasons, his organization approached the company about developing a Mister Rogers attraction at Idlewild.

After considering several concepts, it was decided to re-create a trip through the Neighborhood of Make-Believe with animated figures. The

Mister Rogers' Neighborhood of Make-Believe represented Idlewild's largest expansion when it opened in 1989.

$1 million attraction, located in the thick woods on the south side of Loyalhanna Creek, consists of a 1,600-foot-long trolley ride, which stops at the homes of each of the characters. Children are able to interact with each animated figure. Fred Rogers wrote the script for the attraction, provides the voices, and acts as a creative consultant.

The trolleys are beautiful brass and wood replicas of the trolley on the television show. The cars were not created especially for the park, but were purchased from the Indianapolis Zoo, where they had been built as horse-drawn trolleys. Their weight made them unsuitable for this purpose, and Idlewild was able to purchase them. In a happy coincidence, they were nearly identical to Mr. Rogers' small trolley, and the only necessary modification was the addition of electric motors.

Following the record-breaking 1989 season, Idlewild developed Raccoon Lagoon, located on the south side of Loyalhanna Creek next to Mister Rogers' Neighborhood. At three times the size of the old kiddie area, Raccoon Lagoon provided plenty of room for the nine kiddie rides relocated from the old flood-prone Kiddieland, as well as three new rides, including adult hand cars, which were intended for parents with children too small to operate the kiddie hand cars but are now open to everyone.

Idlewild expanded its water offerings in 1992 with the introduction of Little Squirts, a variety of pools and fountains for small children, in the H2Ohhhh Zone. The following year, the park added its second roller coaster, the Wild Mouse, which was constructed on the site of Idlewild's former Kiddieland. Built by Vekoma of the Netherlands, the ride stands 56 feet high and is 1,640 feet long. Dozens of trees were planted under the roller coaster to obscure its many twists and turns.

Two new rides were introduced in 1998. In Raccoon Lagoon, a lengthy automobile ride called Ricky's Racers joined the lineup of kiddie rides. Idlewild acquired the ride from Old Indiana, a defunct amusement park near Indianapolis, and extensively remodeled it into an all-new attraction. The second ride, named the Tri-nado in a naming contest by local kids, was a large spinning ride.

Idlewild closed out the 1990s with the addition of Dizzy Lizzie's Four Quarters Saloon in Hootin' Holler. The attraction is an updated version of the Haunted Swing, a classic amusement ride dating back to the 1890s, that gives riders the impression that they are turning completely upside down. Idlewild also undertook a major renovation of its sprawling picnic grounds, adding several new rustic log pavilions constructed from trees harvested from park property.

Since it was installed in 1985, the H2Ohhhh Zone had become one of the most popular areas of the park, and on hot summer days, the lines attested to its popularity. In 2000, it was expanded into an all-new water

The water park is an integral part of Idlewild and Soak Zone's diverse lineup of attractions.

area called Soak Zone. Idlewild's largest expansion ever, Soak Zone doubled the size of the water park with six new water slides, a giant bucket holding 300 gallons of water that tips over onto swimmers at regular intervals, water cannons, and a variety of other water features.

Idlewild and Soak Zone Today

While the Idlewild of today is in many respects a modern amusement park, its appeal is timeless. A visitor is greeted with the same relaxed atmosphere in the Laurel Highlands that attracted Thomas Mellon in 1878. Idlewild Park features a total of thirty-four rides, including fourteen for kids, and a full-scale water park. There are seven major areas, each with its own personality.

Olde Idlewild is the original section of the park and includes most of the traditional amusement rides. The more popular rides include the Rollo Coaster and Wild Mouse roller coasters, the antique carousel, and one of the few remaining Caterpillar rides, an old-time classic. Other attractions include miniature golf, midway games, and live shows presented at the Hillside Theater.

Story Book Forest is a large walk-through attraction, with lifesize displays of more than forty well-loved children's stories. Live characters, including the Old Woman in the Shoe and Little Red Riding Hood, inhabit the displays. Children's stories are told in the Puppet Theater.

Hootin' Holler is a re-creation of a Wild West town and is home to most of Idlewild's live shows. Other attractions include Dizzy Lizzie's Four Quarters Saloon, the Confusion Hill illusion attraction, and the Loyalhanna Limited train.

Jumpin' Jungle is a large play area for kids of all ages. Guests can enjoy a 30-foot-high treehouse, a giant net climb, slides, a huge ball pit with 180,000 colored balls, a rope swing, a suspended bridge, a cable slide, and a self-propelled raft ride.

Soak Zone is Idlewild's water park. The park's original swimming pool is at the heart of the area and is complemented by twelve water slides, a variety of water activities, and the Little Squirts play area for kids.

Raccoon Lagoon, located across Loyalhanna Creek, is an 8-acre area devoted to Idlewild's smallest visitors. Among the twelve rides are the Ricky's Racers car ride and scaled-down versions of some of the park's larger attractions, including a Ferris wheel and bumper cars. Look for park mascot Ricky Raccoon. Shows take place at the Raccoon Lagoon Theater.

Mister Rogers' Neighborhood of Make-Believe is located adjacent to Raccoon Lagoon and is home to the trolley ride through the neighborhood. All of the neighbors are here, including King Friday XIII, X the Owl, and Daniel Striped Tiger.

Dorney Park and Wildwater Kingdom

OPENED 1884

IN MANY WAYS, IT'S HARD TO BELIEVE THAT DORNEY PARK AND WILD-water Kingdom is almost 120 years old. Some of the most advanced rides in the industry tower over the landscape, and visitors entering through the modern front entrance are greeted by a gleaming midway lined with restaurants, rides, and games. Nearby, Snoopy and all of his Peanuts friends greet visitors in their own special area. But while much of the park is new, its past is still remembered. Under towering sycamore and poplar trees, planted in 1947 by the former owners, are several nostalgic rides, including a whip. An antique train ride chugs along the creek, next to a classic wooden roller coaster. Dorney Park and Wildwater Kingdom is truly a mix of old and new.

Humble Beginnings

Dorney Park's roots date back to 1860, when Solomon Dorney built a house and fish hatchery at the base of a hill along the banks of Cedar Creek. Located in a grove of trees, it became a primary source of income for Dorney, who sold the fish to area restaurants.

In 1870, Dorney decided that the pastoral setting on the western edge of Allentown was a great place for a weekend getaway, so he added a playground, a small zoo, and refreshment stands. Visitors came from as far as Philadelphia and New York, and Dorney soon added picnic groves, a restaurant in a converted farmhouse, a hotel, a lake created by damming Cedar Creek, and a primitive mechanical ride, the Flying Coaches,

Dorney Park and Wildwater Kingdom

3830 Dorney Park Rd.
Allentown, PA 18104

610-391-7777

www.dorneypark.com

64

which consisted of a cable that ran from high on a pole to the ground. Riders held on to a rope suspended underneath the cable and rode it to ground level.

The operation grew into a full-time business by 1884, when Dorney's Trout Ponds and Summer Resort opened. Consisting largely of the attractions added over the previous fourteen years, the resort continued to build on the reputation that Dorney had established.

Throughout the rest of the nineteenth century, Dorney Park, as it was soon known, continued to add attractions. A theater for concerts and lectures was built on the banks of Cedar Creek, a band shell was constructed, and farmland at the top of the hill was converted into a ball field. Rides were few and mechanically very simple, such as a Venetian Swing, a ride consisting of two-passenger boats suspended underneath a large wooden A-frame in which riders pulled on a rope to make the boat swing back and forth. Cedar Creek remained the center of activity. It was a popular stop for migrating ducks, which soon took up permanent residence and became a symbol of the park.

Trolley Access

In 1899, the Allentown-Kutztown Traction Company, owned by Solomon Dorney's brother C. A., completed a trolley line running from center of Allentown to the park, and eventually to nearby Kutztown. Access to the

Dorney Park's activities in the early years were focused around Cedar Creek.
AUTHOR'S COLLECTION

Even in the early 1900s, water slides were popular at Dorney Park. COLLECTION OF ROBERT OTT

park no longer was limited to horse and carriage. Now a simple nickel streetcar ride brought thousands of visitors.

The increase in business prompted the Traction Company to purchase the park in 1901, following Dorney's death. A crucial addition that season was a brand new carousel. Carved by Gustav Dentzel, the ride featured thirty-six hand-carved animals and was brought in as a concession. As significant as the addition of the carousel was the operator of the ride—Jacob Plarr, a caterer and butcher from Philadelphia. Plarr was a friend of the carousel owner, and his arrival at the park marked the beginning of a ninety-one-year association between Dorney Park and the Plarr family.

The trolley company continued to expand Dorney Park over the next several years, adding larger and more elaborate attractions, such as the Old Mill, in which boats traveled through a dark tunnel, and the Scenic Railway, Dorney's first roller coaster, constructed across the creek from most of the park's attractions. Riders entered through an elaborate two-story pavilion and traveled through several tunnels. In 1920, Plarr installed a whip ride, which remains in operation today as Dorney Park's oldest ride.

An Upgrade

In 1923, the trolley company sold the operation to the Dorney Park Coaster Company, headed by Jacob Plarr's son Robert, who had started working at the park in 1904, at the age of nine. Dorney Park had changed little over the past ten years, and the new owners decided it needed a major upgrade. They arranged for the Philadelphia Toboggan Company (PTC) to add a series of major attractions that would totally transform the park over the next several years.

The first order of business was to build a new roller coaster, as the Scenic Railway had been demolished in 1920 to make way for a new ride. Over the Falls was to be an early version of the log flume, but design

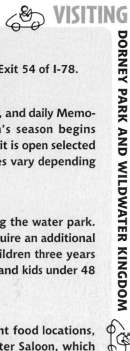

VISITING

DORNEY PARK AND WILDWATER KINGDOM

LOCATION

Dorney Park is located on the west side of Allentown, just off Exit 54 of I-78.

OPERATING SCHEDULE

Dorney Park is open weekends in May, September, and October, and daily Memorial Day weekend through Labor Day. Wildwater Kingdom's season begins Memorial Day weekend and runs through Labor Day, although it is open selected weekends in September. Opening time is 10 A.M.; closing times vary depending on the season.

ADMISSION

One price entitles guests to all rides and attractions, including the water park. The Skyscraper, both go-cart tracks, and the bumper boats require an additional fee, as do parking and games. Admission is less than $40. Children three years and under are free, and there are discounts for senior citizens and kids under 48 inches tall.

FOOD

Dorney Park and Wildwater Kingdom has some forty different food locations, from portable carts to sit-down restaurants, such as Red Garter Saloon, which offers live entertainment throughout the day. Coasters Drive-In, a 1950s style burger joint, provides cafeteria service, and there are also several fast-food franchises. Although you are not permitted to bring food into Dorney Park and Wildwater Kingdom, there is a public picnic area next to the entrance.

FOR CHILDREN

Camp Snoopy is the main kids' area, with nine family rides in a north-woods environment. Keep an eye out for your favorite Peanuts characters. Also look for Chuck's Lunch Box, which serves kid favorites like macaroni and cheese.

Tot Spot, located along Cedar Creek, is a more traditional kiddie area, with seven rides, including two roller coasters.

Whitewater Kingdom is home to two kid's play areas—Lollipop Lagoon and Kids' Cove.

There are also a number of rides for the whole family, including the antique carousel, a newer merry-go-round, two train rides, the Road Rally auto ride, the giant Ferris wheel, and the Thunder Creek Mountain flume.

SPECIAL FEATURES

Dorney Park is home to six major roller coasters, including Steel Force, rated one of the best roller coasters in the world and the largest in Pennsylvania; Talon, a modern looping thriller; Laser, a more traditional looping ride; Hercules, one of the world's largest wooden roller coasters; Thunderhawk, a classic twisting woody; and Wild Mouse, a family ride.

(continued on page 68)

VISITING (continued from page 67)

Don't miss the antique Dentzel carousel, one of the finest examples of the carousel art, and Dorney Park's classic antique rides—the Zephyr train, along Cedar Creek, and the whip, one of the last rides of its kind.

TIME REQUIRED

Dorney Park and Wildwater Kingdom is easily a full-day outing, and it could take two days to experience everything. Both one- and two-day tickets are available.

TOURING TIPS

Admission prices are lower in the evening and during weekends before Memorial Day and after Labor Day.

Arrive at the park about a half hour before opening, as sometimes the gates open early. Head to Steel Force and enjoy the attractions in this back area of the park, then work your way toward the front.

Try visiting on a weekday, or on a weekend in May or September; crowds tend to be lighter.

problems halted construction. Instead, a new roller coaster, simply called Coaster, opened in 1924. It was a large ride, standing 72 feet tall and having a top speed of 63 miles per hour. A bumper car building was constructed next to the loading station of the roller coaster.

Another signature attraction from PTC was added to Dorney Park in 1927, when the Mill Chute was built next to the Coaster. The immensely popular Mill Chute featured a boat ride through a dark tunnel that ended with a plunge down a roller-coaster-type drop into a large pool.

The Coaster was reconfigured in 1930 to compete with other parks, which were adding larger thrill rides. PTC lengthened the ride to 2,767 feet, increased its height to 80 feet, and converted its straight hills into twisting drops. The ride was a huge hit and remained a favorite among roller coaster enthusiasts for decades.

Even during the Depression, Dorney Park continued to expand. In 1932, a decision was made to replace the original carousel. Although it still had great sentimental value for the Plarrs, the animals did not go up and down like more modern carousels, which hurt its popularity. Other parks were shutting down by the dozens, and Dorney Park was able to obtain a carousel that had been repossessed by PTC when Shellpot Park in Delaware closed. The new carousel was seventeen years old, but it represented one of PTC's best works, featuring twenty-eight jumping horses, eighteen standing horses, and two chariots. It was placed in a new building in the heart of Dorney Park.

In 1935, the park made a crucial decision to construct a new ride. This was unheard of during the tough economic times, especially since trolley service to the park had ceased that year. The famous Burlington Railroad Zephyr train and its high-speed runs through the American West captivated the country during this era, and the park hired a local mechanical engineer to construct a miniature replica of the train. It featured a unique drive system in which a gasoline engine in the front of the train drove an electric motor between each car, which in turn drove the wheels. Since this was such a novelty, people flocked to Dorney Park to see it, providing sufficient revenues to keep the park in operation through the remainder of the Depression. It remains a favorite attraction and still retains its original motors.

America was absorbed with World War II during the 1940s, and Dorney Park's priorities shifted to the war effort. To help alleviate food shortages, the park sold its famous ducks for food, raised capons and turkeys, which were also sold, in the skating rink, and converted the Castle Garden ballroom into a USO facility.

Not every idea worked well. In the early 1950s, Dorney Park converted one of its lakes into a fish-and-pay concession. But the fish proved too cooperative, and it soon turned into a money loser. Robert Ott, who worked at the park from 1937 to 1985, recalls Robert Plarr telling him, "They're catching too many fish . . . we have to stop that!" He ordered Ott to feed the fish at night after the park closed. But the fish were hungry again by morning and continued to cooperate with patrons, and the attraction was soon phased out.

The 1935 opening of the Zephyr train helped save Dorney Park during the Depression.

More Changes

In 1960, noted amusement park designer William Tracy created an elaborate facade for the roller coaster–bumper car building to serve as a park entrance. It was topped by a giant clown that was given the name Alfundo, for "*Al*lentown has *Fun* at *Do*rney," who became the park mascot.

Tracy returned in 1961 to renovate the Mill Chute into Journey to the Center of the Earth, adding another elaborate facade and a series of scenes in the tunnel. In 1962, he renovated the old Devil's Cave dark ride, which was built in 1937, into Pirate's Cove dark ride. But 1962 also marked the end of one of Dorney's most enduring traditions, as the pool was closed after sixty-one years. Not only did the aging pool need a new filtration system, but new health regulations required that the pool's sand bottom be replaced with cement.

Dorney Park could not justify the cost to totally remove the pool, so for the 1963 season, the park split the pool down the middle, placing a boat ride in one half and using the other half as the focal point of the new Zoorama attraction. Sea lions were housed in the pool, a hippopotamus lived in the former wading pool, and the bathhouse was converted into a menagerie building with a hundred animals.

Dorney Park Road still ran through the center of the park in the early 1970s. PHOTO BY ROBERT OTT

On August 15, 1964, fire struck the Zoorama. A quick-thinking park attendant used a jeep to break down the wall of the former bathhouse to evacuate the animals. Meanwhile, the hippo dove underwater and held its breath until the fire was put out. As a result, only a few animals lost their lives, but the building was a total loss. In the truest show-business spirit, an all-new Zoorama was ready for the 1965 season.

The park achieved international recognition in 1967 when the movie *Where Angels Go . . . Trouble Follows,* starring Rosalind Russell and Stella Stevens, was filmed at the park. On the day of the filming, customers started arriving at the park as early as 8 A.M., prompting Dorney to open four hours early. Though Dorney Park was featured for only a few minutes in the movie, it provided priceless publicity for the park. "The final shoot was a picture of Alfundo and our front entrance," remembers Robert Ott. "You couldn't buy that publicity!"

The 1970s were a decade of change for Dorney Park. They started with the addition of four new rides. In 1973, a fire destroyed the Wacky Shack dark ride, which had opened in the former skating rink in 1964. But in 1977, the park was able to acquire 15 acres adjacent to the park in a land swap with Lehigh County that permitted a major midway and parking lot expansion. Covering 4 acres, the new midway contained a theater, a variety of concessions, and the Flying Dutchman, billed as the world's largest portable roller coaster. The $500,000 ride was placed at the top of the hill, providing an instant landmark, standing 70 feet tall and featuring a 50-foot first drop and 3,240 feet of track.

America was talking about energy rationing in 1978, and Dorney Park experimented with alternative energy by adding the Windjammer 475, the most powerful private wind turbine in the country. The 101-foot-tall windmill was supposed to generate 225,000 watts of electricity, 10 to 15 percent of the park's energy needs. But according to Robert Ott, "We received international attention for installing it, but unfortunately, it never worked right." It was soon removed.

In 1979, after an eleven-year effort, the park was able to close Dorney Park Road, a road that had divided the park since the beginning, forcing patrons to cross the street to get from one portion to the other. With the road eliminated, Dorney Park was fenced in, and admission was charged for the first time in 1982. Despite some initial grumbling, park revenue increased and generated the funds needed to totally upgrade the facility. New entrances were built and restrooms were renovated, but more significantly, Dorney Park added its largest ride ever. The park took on debt for the first time to add a $1.5 million log flume. Dubbed Thunder Creek Mountain, the 1,230-foot-long ride was constructed on the 56-foot-high hillside where the park's deer herd once roamed.

The Park's Hundredth Anniversary

Dorney Park's hundredth anniversary was rapidly approaching, and a huge celebration was planned for the 1984 season. Over its first century, the park had faced many challenges, and it had survived them all, but on September 21, 1983, it was presented with its greatest challenge yet. As the park was preparing to close for winter, a fire broke out in a refreshment stand. A heavy wind created an inferno, and firefighters converged on the park to battle the blaze. When it was extinguished two hours later, the heart of the park had been destroyed.

Ten acres had been affected. Gone were four refreshment stands, two theaters, the Bucket of Blood dark ride, and the Flying Bobs. Most painful was the loss of the magnificent old carousel, the centerpiece of Dorney Park for fifty-one years, which was reduced to a pile of ashes. The total loss was estimated at $3 million.

But the park was fully insured, and cleanup and reconstruction quickly began. Amazingly, the park managed to open for its hundredth anniversary season on schedule, with barely any evidence of the fire. And the reconstruction allowed the park to improve its layout and update much of its infrastructure.

"Disneyland of the Northeast"

On May 22, 1985, Robert Ott retired after nearly fifty years at Dorney Park and sold his family's 50 percent interest to Harris Weinstein, who was married to Deborah Plarr, Jacob's great-granddaughter. Weinstein had big plans for the park. Seeing that 60 million people lived within a day's drive of the park, he announced that Dorney Park would be transformed into the "Disneyland of the Northeast."

As a start, on June 15, 1985, Wildwater Kingdom opened for business. Constructed by Dorney Park as a separate attraction, Wildwater Kingdom was located at the top of the hill and separated from the amusement park by a parking lot. Among its attractions were the third-largest wave pool in the world, six water slides, and a variety of water play elements.

As with any change in ownership, some traditions end. The racetrack, which replaced the hilltop ball field in 1939, was closed after the 1986 season. The famous Dorney ducks were removed. Alfundo was retired in 1988. Finally, with the prices of antique carousels skyrocketing, the original 1901 Dentzel machine, which had been brought out of storage for occasional special events, was sold to raise funds for park expansion.

Important additions were made as well. Weinstein kicked off his tenure at Dorney Park by adding Laser, a $2.5 million, 2,200-foot-long, steel-track roller coaster featuring two 90-foot-tall loops built on the former site of the Zoorama, which closed in 1983.

Attendance in 1986 increased nearly 20 percent. This success prompted Weinstein to continue his aggressive expansion. In 1987, the park received a new modern merry-go-round, and Wildwater Kingdom received a $3.5 million Runaway River ride, in which riders traveled on inner tubes down a 1,400-foot-long river, the largest ride of its kind.

Weinstein was just getting started. Visitors to the park in 1988 were greeted by $10 million worth of improvements, including a new $7 million area on the site of the former racetrack, called the Flight Deck. This area featured four new rides, a restaurant, and a 3,500-seat theater called the Stargazer Showplace.

Intent on putting itself on the national map, Dorney Park jumped into the roller coaster arms race with both feet in 1989 by constructing Hercules, the world's largest wooden roller coaster. Anchoring the Flight Deck area, Hercules took advantage of the hillside where the deer formerly roamed to build a 157-foot drop, 16 feet taller than any other wooden roller coaster drop, even though the ride itself stood just 95 feet tall. The $6 million, 4,000-foot-long ride was built by the Dinn Corporation of Cincinnati, the leading roller coaster builder of the 1980s.

The park also spent $9 million for additional improvements, which included replacing the Flying Dutchman with a 100-foot-tall Ferris wheel. Three additional water slides and Lollipop Lagoon, a special kids' area, were added to Wildwater Kingdom.

Dorney Park and Hercules achieved national headlines of a different sort following the 1989 season, when Six Flags Over Texas in Arlington announced construction of what they claimed would be the world's tallest wooden roller coaster. Though their 143-foot-tall ride was actually taller than the 95-foot-tall Hercules, Hercules's hillside location gave it a larger maximum drop, 157 feet versus Six Flags' 137 feet. As a result, each park claimed its roller coaster was the tallest. In an interview with the Allentown *Morning Call,* Harris Weinstein said, "No one really cares how high a structure is; what they do care about is the height of the drop, that's what they really experience." Six Flags countered by stating, "Roller coasters are judged by the height of the first lift and the structure supporting it. We feel ours is the tallest wooden roller coaster structure around."

On March 30, 1990, Dorney Park filed suit in federal court asking that Six Flags cease all advertising claiming that their roller coaster was the tallest in the world. Industry observers were stunned by this unprecedented action. As the trial was set to start, the two parks reached an agreement in which each park acknowledged the other's claim—Dorney Park had the highest drop of any wooden roller coaster, and Six Flags Over Texas had the highest hill. But within two years, Fiesta Texas in San Antonio beat them both, with a 181-foot-tall roller coaster featuring

Hercules had the largest drop on any wooden roller coaster when it opened in 1989. PHOTO BY CEDAR FAIR LP

a 166-foot drop. In the end, the general manager of Six Flags Over Texas told *Amusement Business* magazine, "Probably the only people who benefited were the lawyers."

Soon, larger roller coasters were being constructed around the country, and the park briefly considered adding 27 feet to Hercules's structure to increase the height of its drop to 185 feet to reclaim the world record, but it was decided to invest funds elsewhere. The $1.4 million Aquablast water slide, at 66 feet tall and 701 feet long advertised as "the largest, tallest and steepest tube slide in the world," debuted in 1991.

Continued Growth

By the beginning of 1992, Harris Weinstein had run Dorney Park and Wildwater Kingdom for seven years. During that time, he had transformed Dorney Park from a small, local amusement park into a regional facility, spending $60 million and increasing attendance from four hundred thousand to 1.5 million. That accomplishment did not go unnoticed, and on January 23, 1992, Cedar Fair Limited Partnership announced that it had reached an agreement to purchase Dorney Park and Wildwater Kingdom. Cedar Fair is a publicly held company that had achieved fame by purchasing Cedar Point, a dying amusement park in Sandusky, Ohio, in 1956 and transforming it into the largest and arguably most successful amusement resort in the Midwest. Like Weinstein, they saw that Dorney Park had tremendous potential with the large number of people living nearby.

After several months of negotiations, Cedar Fair completed its $48 million acquisition of Dorney Park and Wildwater Kingdom on July 22, 1992. In keeping with the company's strategy that "you have to spend money to make it," Cedar Fair announced plans to spend $25 million to improve the park over the next five years.

Cedar Fair kicked off its expansion program with $8 million in improvements for the 1993 season. Several of the old rides were removed, and the former Flight Deck area was transformed into a Western-themed area. The main attraction was White Water Landing, billed as the largest waterfall plunge in the world. Riders seated in twelve-passenger boats traveled up an 80-foot hill, rounded a turn, and dropped into a pond at 42 miles per hour, producing a 25-foot-high splash. Next door was the Cedar Creek Cannonball, a new train ride that connected the amusement park and the water park.

Development of this area continued in 1994 with the addition of Thunder Canyon, a river rapids ride in which round, eight-person boats traveled down a 1,640-foot-long channel, where they were assaulted by eight geysers and fourteen waterfalls. In the older portion of Dorney Park, buildings were upgraded, and the Road Rally turnpike ride was built on the former site of the Journey to the Center of the Earth mill chute ride.

Dorney Park and Wildwater Kingdom became a single, unified attraction in 1995 as a result of a new $5.5 million entrance that linked the two facilities. Serving as a new focal point of the entrance was a magnificent antique carousel relocated from Cedar Point. William Dentzel of Philadelphia originally built the carousel in 1921. It features sixty-eight hand-carved animals, including a deer, a lion, a tiger, a giraffe, and fifty jumping horses. The carousel is considered such a fine example of carousel art that it was added to the National Register of Historic Places in 1990. Berenstain Bear Country, an all-new children's area featuring eight interactive play areas, also helped fill the former gap between the amusement park and water park.

World-class roller coasters are a signature of Cedar Fair's parks, and Dorney Park announced that after three years of planning, a new roller coaster would dominate the landscape in 1997. Costing $10 million, the new ride, named Steel Force, was built along the entire southern border of the park. Dwarfing its older brother, Thunderhawk, Steel Force towers 200 feet tall and is 5,600 feet long. Riders travel 76 miles per hour over a 205-foot first drop into a 120-foot-long tunnel. At the far end of the ride, the trains travel through a high-speed spiral. Built by the California firm of D.

H. Morgan, Steel Force remains the largest roller coaster in Pennsylvania, and in its first year of operation it immediately became a favorite of roller coaster enthusiasts.

Dorney Park continued to grow as the 1990s came to an end. The entrance was further developed with the addition of Coasters restaurant and Hang Time, a 59-foot-tall ride that takes riders on a flipping, twisting journey. The 1,200-foot-long Thunder Creek Speedway was built under Steel Force, and the Island Water Works, a three-story structure featuring seventy differ-

Steel Force, built in 1997, towers over its older brother, the 1930 vintage Thunderhawk.

Dominator took Dorney Park to new heights when it opened in 1999. PHOTO BY CEDAR FAIR LP

ent water elements, was constructed in the water park.

The central portion of the park received most of the attention in 1999, with the addition of Dominator, a 200-foot-tall tower featuring two different rides. One ride shoots riders up 160 feet in less than three seconds, and the other slowly takes them 175 feet to the top and shoots them down at more than 40 miles per hour.

Though Cedar Fair had already spent over $50 million to improve Dorney Park and Wildwater Kingdom since acquiring it, the year 2000 saw an additional $12.5 million worth of improvements. Much of the money was spent to convert Berenstain Bear Country into Camp Snoopy, a 2-acre area that resembles a north-woods campground but is full of rides for the entire family, with a scaled-down roller coaster, Woodstock Express, and eight other family rides. Also added were the Wild Mouse, a modern version of the roller coaster that thrilled patrons at Dorney Park from the 1950s until the early 1970s, and Skyscraper, a 150-foot arm with two seats at either end that spins head over heels, reaching speeds of 60 miles per hour.

Talon, another signature roller coaster, greeted visitors at the front gate in 2001. Riders are suspended underneath the track, rather than traveling above, and are flipped upside down four times, at speeds of up to 58 miles per hour. Built by the renowned Swiss firm of Bolliger & Mabilliard, the $14 million ride towers 135 feet over the park and features a maximum drop of 120 feet.

Dorney Park and Wildwater Kingdom Today

Today, Dorney Park and Wildwater Kingdom features a total of fifty-two rides—a mix of old and new—including fourteen for kids, a full-scale water park, and a variety of other attractions. At the entrance area are

Dorney Park's antique Dentzel carousel, Coasters restaurant, a wide array of games and concessions, and two of Dorney Park's roller coasters—the Wild Mouse for families and Talon, the park's newest high-speed thriller.

Immediately to the right of the front entrance is Wildwater Kingdom. A complete water park, it features eleven water slides of every description, two river rides, a 750,000-gallon wave pool, and Island Waterworks, a huge play area with seventy water-based activities. There are two play areas just for kids, Lollipop Lagoon and Kids' Cove.

The entrance area leads to Dorney Park's Western area, which has two water rides—Thunder Canyon and White Water Landing—along with the Hercules roller coaster and Red Garter Saloon, offering food and live entertainment. A laser show is presented nightly.

Next door, visitors are greeted by the Peanuts characters at Camp Snoopy, which features nine rides for kids and their families, including Woodstock Express, a junior-size roller coaster.

The main park area, leading down the hill to Cedar Creek, is where the majority of the rides and attractions are located, including the Giant Wheel, Dominator, Thunder Creek Mountain, and the Laser and Steel Force roller coasters, along with Tot Spot, which features seven kiddie rides. Live shows take place at Center Stage, next to Dominator. This is the oldest part of Dorney Park and is home to its oldest attractions—the whip, Thunderhawk roller coaster, and Zephyr train.

Conneaut Lake Community Park

OPENED 1892

AS IN MANY OTHER TOWNS, CONNEAUT LAKE PARK'S MAIN STREET, PARK Avenue, was the heart of the town's activity. But a drive down Park Avenue revealed a town like no other. Interspersed with the houses were not businesses, but a miniature train and a roller coaster. The town's main intersection of Park Avenue and Comstock Street featured, in addition to a restaurant on one corner, a bumper car ride, a carousel, and midway games on the other corners. This wasn't just any town, but the town of Conneaut Lake Park.

Times change. The streets where cars once traveled have been closed to traffic and are now midways traversing the amusement park. But the turn-of-the-century charm remains, from the huge trees lining the streets to the nostalgic rides that remain favorites. The sprawling Victorian resort hotel and the boardwalk along the shore of Pennsylvania's largest natural lake create an atmosphere that is truly special.

The Exposition Park Years

Like many of Pennsylvania's other amusement parks, Conneaut Lake Community Park was a popular gathering place for many years before it officially opened. In 1877, Aaron Lynce purchased 7 acres on the eastern shore of Conneaut Lake and opened a boat landing. After enjoying success for a number of years, Lynce sold his land in 1892 to the Conneaut Lake Exposition Company, which had been formed in April 1892 by Col. Frank Mantor after visiting Williams Grove Park

> **Conneaut Lake Community Park**
> 12382 Center St.
> Conneaut Lake, PA 16316
> 814-382-5115
> or 877-782-5115
> www.conneautlakepark.com

The grassy lakefront area known as the Commons remains a center of activity at Conneaut Lake Park. AUTHOR'S COLLECTION

near Harrisburg. Mantor came up with a plan for a permanent fairground exhibiting livestock, machinery, and industrial products from western Pennsylvania. He also planned to include a series of lectures and classes. Upon returning to northwest Pennsylvania after his visit to Harrisburg, he recruited investors, including the Pittsburgh & Shenango Valley Railroad, which promised to extend its rail line into the park. The Exposition Company purchased Lynce's land and 175 acres of adjacent land, 75 of which were given to Lynce as payment for his parcel.

By August 15, 1892, Exposition Park, as it was then known, was ready for business. Promoted as the "Queen of All Inland Summer Resorts," the new resort featured a convention hall for lectures and concerts, dancing, and a bathing beach with an elaborate bathhouse. Most of the structures from Lynce's Landing were retained, and a farmhouse on the property was converted into the Echo Hotel. During those early years, there was no road access to the park, and all visitors had to arrive by train or boat from the town of Conneaut Lake.

Several new structures were added for Exposition Park's second season, including the Exposition Hotel on the site of Lynce's lakefront home, a sixteen-hundred-seat auditorium, and two exhibition halls. Most of the

VISITING

LOCATION

Conneaut Lake Community Park is located about 10 miles west of I-79 on PA Route 618. Take Exit 147B of I-79 onto U.S. Route 6 West to Route 618 North.

OPERATING SCHEDULE

Conneaut Lake Community Park is open Memorial Day weekend through Labor Day. It opens at noon daily, except Monday and Tuesday, when it is closed. The Hotel Conneaut and the Beach Club are open through the fall for special events.

ADMISSION

Parking and admission to Conneaut Lake Community Park are free. You can either pay by the ride or purchase a Combo Pass for under $20 that entitles you to all rides and attractions, including the water park. The paddle-wheel boat, live ponies, games, and miniature golf cost extra.

FOOD

Conneaut Lake Community Park has nearly twenty different food locations, from portable carts to the Hotel Conneaut dining room. Most of the smaller stands are clustered along the midway near the lakefront. Food is also available in the Beach Club. You may bring your own food into the park. Picnic pavilions are available on a first-come, first-served basis.

FOR CHILDREN

The self-contained kiddieland features eleven rides, including a roller coaster, live ponies, a play area, games, and a food facility. Conneaut Lake Community Park also has a large number of classic family rides, including the Tumble Bug, train, Flying Scooter, and carousel.

SPECIAL FEATURES

There are few amusement parks in the world that can match Conneaut Lake Community Park's laid-back, old-fashioned atmosphere. From the towering trees to the 600-foot-long lakefront boardwalk, the waterfront Beach Club, and the nostalgic hotel with its large porch, this place is special.

Conneaut Lake Community Park is also home to an extensive array of vintage amusement park rides that are rare in today's amusement parks. These include one of only three Tumble Bug rides remaining in operation, a Flying Scooter ride, the Twister, the Devil's Den, a one-of-a-kind gravity-powered dark ride, the carousel, and the Blue Streak roller coaster. The kiddieland also features a number of lovingly maintained classics from the 1950s.

(continued on page 82)

CONNEAUT LAKE PARK

VISITING (continued from page 81)

TIME REQUIRED

If your time is limited, Conneaut Lake Community Park can be experienced in about four hours, but to truly take advantage of everything the park has to offer, plan on spending an entire day.

TOURING TIPS

Crowds tend to be lighter on weekdays, when the park offers a discounted Combo Pass. Combo Passes are also discounted in the evening.

buildings were clustered around the Commons, a large, grassy area along the lakefront that still exists as Conneaut Lake Community Park's concert area.

Through the 1890s, Exposition Park evolved as a combination small town and fairground, with exhibition halls and hotels lining the streets. They were joined by a variety of small businesses hoping to capitalize on the traffic. Summer cottages were also interspersed among the larger buildings. This early period gave the park its personality, which remains to this day.

Exposition Park received its first mechanical ride in 1899. A steam-powered carousel was brought to the park by the T. M. Harton Company of Pittsburgh, which, during the early part of the century, was a leading builder of amusement parks and attractions.

The Hotel Conneaut is the soul of Conneaut Lake Community Park.

Conneaut Lake Park had a small-town atmosphere even in its earliest days.
AUTHOR'S COLLECTION

The railroad took control of Exposition Park in 1901, and a period of substantial growth followed. Featuring nearly a dozen hotels, it became one of the largest resorts in the region. In 1902, Fred Ingersoll, another noted developer of amusement parks and attractions from Pittsburgh, built the park's first roller coaster, the Figure Eight. Also during this time, the Exposition Hotel was gradually rebuilt into the Hotel Conneaut, still the focal point of the park's lakefront activities. The addition of trolley service from nearby Meadville in 1907 further increased Exposition Park's appeal. The resort was firmly established. The railroad advertised the park as "free from malaria, hay fever, and other summer ills, realizing a refreshing sleep, regaining strength, and reluctantly leaving at the end of vacation, better prepared to battle life's struggles in counting house, office or shop."

Just when all seemed to be going well, disaster struck. On December 2, 1908, over half of the park was destroyed when a fire broke out in the Hotel Bismarck, located in the northwestern portion of the park. Wind swept the fire east toward the lake, burning the Old Mill, the dance hall, four additional hotels, the boat landing, the Figure Eight roller coaster, the bowling alley, and a variety of smaller businesses. The Hotel Conneaut and Hotel Virginia, which opened in 1906, narrowly escaped damage.

Some might have viewed this as a crushing blow, but Exposition Park took advantage of the opportunity to rebuild along Park Avenue, using cement block instead of wood. Many of these buildings still stand at the park today, including what was then the bowling alley and the Dreamland Ballroom, billed as the largest ballroom between New York and Chicago, with a 20,000-square-foot dance floor. A new Figure Eight roller coaster was constructed, as was the Scenic Railway, another major

The carousel building has been a fixture at the corner of Park Avenue and Comstock Street since 1910.

roller coaster. The next season, the park's current carousel made its debut. Built by T. M. Harton, it was placed in an elaborate new carousel building at the corner of Park Avenue and Comstock Street.

Conneaut Lake Park

In 1920, the park's name was changed to Conneaut Lake Park, as the fairground attractions were increasingly deemphasized. The decade was spent expanding the ride lineup. In 1922, the Figure Eight was modernized and renamed the Jack Rabbit; a bumper car ride was installed in 1923; and 1925 saw the addition of the Tumble Bug, a large ride with circular cars traveling on an undulating track.

In 1927, trolley service to Conneaut Lake Park ended. The loss of patronage, combined with increasing competition from other amusement parks as well as from movies, forced the park into receivership on September 27, 1929. For the next three seasons, Conneaut Lake Park struggled in the face of absentee owners and the Depression. By October 1932, it looked as though the park was headed for liquidation. But because of the Depression, it was concluded that no one would have the resources to purchase any of Conneaut Lake Park's assets, and that it would have to be sold as a going concern. As a result, one of the two banks controlling the park, the Crawford County Trust Company, was permitted by the court to foreclose on the park, but the other bank, the People's Pittsburgh Trust, appealed, and Conneaut Lake Park was allowed to remain open for one more year. In November 1933, Conneaut Lake Park was auctioned off, and People's Pittsburgh Trust purchased the park for $35,000.

Although the bank did not want to be in the amusement park business, it also did not want to lose its investment. When the park was faced with the discontinuation of regular railroad service in 1934, the bank installed new management. It also built a new water system, including a 130-foot-tall water tower that remains a park landmark.

Other new features that are still favorites among park goers today soon followed. In 1935, the park's original bathhouse was replaced by the Beach Club, a lakefront nightclub, and a 600-foot-long boardwalk extending from the Beach Club to the Hotel Conneaut opened in 1936.

The bank's management was truly making progress in turning the operation around. For the 1938 season, the Jack Rabbit was torn down and five new rides were added. Most notable was an all-new roller coaster that replaced the Scenic Railway, the Blue Streak, built by Edward Vettel, another noted roller coaster designer from Pittsburgh. The new ride was constructed through the woods parallel to Park Avenue, and at 77 feet tall, it made its presence known throughout the park as it roared through the woods.

Conneaut Lake Park added one of the first Tumble Bug rides in 1925. It remains a favorite.

In 1943, lightning struck the Hotel Conneaut and started a fire that destroyed half the hotel. Because of World War II–related rationing, it was not possible to fully rebuild the hotel, which had had 300 rooms, and in 1945, it reopened in its current 133-room configuration. Fortunately, the fire did not set back the progress that the bank's management group had made over the previous decade, and by 1944, Conneaut Lake Park was purchased out of bankruptcy by an investor group led by Dr. Harry Winslow, a local surgeon.

The first new rides since the start of the war—a Tilt-A-Whirl and a Ferris wheel—debuted in 1949. In 1950, the Castle of Fun, in the former bowling alley, was replaced by the Crazy Maze. With the postwar baby boom in full force, Conneaut Lake Park spent the next several seasons building up their kiddie ride lineup, including a kiddie roller coaster in 1954.

Conneaut Lake Park took advantage of the popularity of automobile travel and the baby boom in 1960 by turning several acres across the

The Beach Club has been a fixture on the shores of Conneaut Lake since 1935.

main highway from the park into Fairyland Forest. Like many similar attractions opening throughout the country during the time, Fairyland Forest featured lifesize displays of beloved children's stories and a petting zoo with a hundred animals. In 1961, the Blue Streak was joined by another roller coaster, the Wild Mouse, and the Crazy Maze was converted into a fun house.

By now, the latest rage sweeping America was the huge, carefully planned, corporate-owned theme parks, with their groundbreaking rides. Taking a page from one of the most famous of these new theme park rides, Conneaut Lake Park introduced the Jungle Cruise in 1962. A takeoff on the famous Disney attraction, the Jungle Cruise featured boats that traveled through canals behind the Blue Streak to view displays of both live and mechanical animals.

Unlike the hard times many other amusement parks were experiencing during this era, Conneaut Lake Park, with its resort atmosphere, continued to thrive. In 1968, the Devils Den, a gravity-powered dark ride, made its debut. Paying homage to its roots, in 1972, the park introduced paddle-wheel boat tours of Conneaut Lake aboard the *Barbara J.* A second dark ride joined the lineup in 1974, originally called the Pit of Death, but changed to Dracula's Cave the following season.

David versus Goliath

On the surface, it appeared that Conneaut Lake Park was holding its own in a changing world. The ride lineup was growing, and the last remaining hotel, the Hotel Conneaut, remained a popular retreat. Beneath the surface, however, all was not well. The owners were having disagreements about the future of the park, and in 1974, Dr. John and Mary Gene Winslow Flynn, the son-in-law and daughter of Dr. Winslow, bought out the other partners, saddling the park with $750,000 in debt.

The debt slowed expansion. The Ultimate Trip, an enclosed Scrambler ride with a light and sound show, replaced the fun house in 1976. But Conneaut Lake Park was struggling. Much of the region was mired in a deep recession, and Conneaut Lake Park was losing many of its industrial picnics. A new perspective was needed. As a result, the Flynns asked their son Charles for help. Employed in New York City government, he was looking for new challenges and was intrigued by the potential of Conneaut Lake Park. He immediately went to work to rejuvenate the family business. Expansion in 1981 focused on traditional rides, and a new Paratrooper and Yo Yo swing ride were added. Improvements shifted to the lakefront the following season, with the Rampage, a new slide into the lake, and the beginning of a five-year renovation of the

Conneaut Lake Park's main street, Park Avenue, before the park was fenced in 1990.

Hotel Conneaut. In addition, for the first time ever, the Blue Streak was actually painted blue.

In 1986, Charles Flynn capped his fifth year at Conneaut Lake Park by making two important additions to the amusement park. Along Park Avenue, Cliffhanger Falls, a 48-foot-tall water slide tower with two 415-foot-long slides, replaced the giant slide and the Dracula's Cave dark ride. The appeal of Fairyland Forest had been declining for several years, so Flynn decided to use the property for Camperland, a campground with 105 sites.

Flynn had succeeded in stabilizing Conneaut Lake Park, but running a small, family-owned amusement park in the theme-park era was a constant challenge. Insurance costs kept rising, aging rides and buildings needed renovations, and new attractions kept increasing in cost. With prices for antique carousel horses skyrocketing, Conneaut Lake Park made the difficult decision to sell some of the antique figures from its carousel. Rather than purchase mass-produced fiberglass replacements, the park contracted with Carousel Works of Mansfield, Ohio, to craft one-of-a-kind wooden replacements. On June 25, 1989, Conneaut Lake Park rededicated its carousel. Using the proceeds from the sale of the carousel animals, the seventy-nine-year-old ride was completely refurbished. Nineteen new hand-carved figures joined the twenty-nine original horses that were retained. An antique band organ was purchased to provide music, and eighteen original oil paintings depicting the history of the region were mounted on the carousel. Other proceeds were used to renovate the kiddieland with new cement walkways and Victorian gazebos.

Attendance in 1989 reached three hundred thousand, 50 percent higher than when Charles Flynn took over in 1981, but revenues still were not enough to offset increasing expenses. Flynn made a watershed decision. Starting in 1990, the streets that ran through the amusement park would be closed to traffic, the park would be fenced, and admission would be charged. To many, it seemed a drastic action that robbed Conneaut Lake Park of much of its appeal. But in a letter to customers explaining the change, Flynn stated, "Traditional parks are dropping like flies and it's time we all realize that we have to take steps now and save our park before its too late to do anything about it."

Conneaut Lake Park had high hopes for the 1990 season. Visitors were greeted by an elaborate new Victorian-themed main entrance, an extensive lineup of live entertainment was introduced, and a jeep-drawn tram ride purchased in Atlantic City hauled visitors throughout the grounds.

Despite an aggressive public-relations campaign, the season was a disaster. The public was slow to accept the changes, and only two weekends the entire summer were without rain. To cut costs and raise cash, six rides were sold in 1991, including the Wild Mouse and the Ferris wheel. The proceeds were spent on improvements. The park added Otter Creek River Adventure, a 650-foot-long river ride next to the water slides. The Dreamland Ballroom, which had been used as a warehouse for several years, was reopened for dances and special events. The improvements were well received, attendance increased, and Conneaut Lake Park looked ahead to its hundredth anniversary in 1992 with optimism.

But poor weather again led to poor attendance. Flynn decided there was little hope for the park to succeed in its current format, and in August, he announced that all of the rides, except the train, bumper cars, carousel, and kiddie rides, would be sold. The water park would be expanded, and Conneaut Lake Park would focus on special events, concerts, group picnics, and nonride activities, such as batting cages, mazes, and sports activities. The famous Blue Streak roller coaster, which needed a $100,000 renovation, would be mothballed. At the time, park owner Charles Flynn told *Amusement Business* magazine, "It's fun to play David and Goliath for a while, but only in the Bible does David win."

The announced changes deeply concerned many area residents, especially since it was projected that one hundred thousand fewer people would come to the park each year. As a result, several local businessmen approached Flynn about purchasing the park, but it was too late to stop the auction of the rides.

On the day of auction, more than two hundred potential buyers and curious onlookers from around the country showed up. A New Jersey carnival took home the whip; the Spider was sold to an Ohio-based carnival; the tram was sold to Old Indiana, a theme park near Indianapolis; and a Harley-Davidson dealer purchased the kiddie merry-go-round. As the day went on, the same person kept surfacing as the winning bidder for most of the rides, but no one in the crowd knew who he was. Finally, toward the end of the auction, it was revealed that a group of four local businessmen was in negotiations to purchase the park and keep it intact. By the end of the auction, they had managed to purchase eleven of the seventeen rides for sale.

Trying to Find a Niche

By early 1993, the sale of Conneaut Lake Park was finalized. The new owners were optimistic about the future. A series of concession buildings along the lake dating back to 1909 were demolished to expand the Commons for an expanded lineup of concerts and festivals, $200,000 was spent upgrading rides, and numerous flowers and shrubs were planted. But there were only twenty-two rides, half the number in operation just ten years earlier, and many in the area thought that the park had closed altogether. Attendance dropped to 278,000.

Writing the year off as a learning experience, the owners brought in a new management team for 1994, and two rides were added. But the public again was unresponsive to the changes, and attendance plunged to 225,000.

After racking up nearly $1 million in losses over the two seasons, the owners were forced to file for bankruptcy in early 1995. Attempts to sell the park were unsuccessful, and for the first time, Conneaut Lake Park failed to open for the summer in 1995. A local family, remembering the happy times they had at the park, set up the Conneaut Lake Preservation Fund to try to rescue the park. They held a benefit concert, promoted the park's plight, and set the goal to raise $3 million. But they were able to raise only $25,000.

As 1995 dragged into 1996, no buyers had surfaced, and the outlook for the park grew darker. Just when it appeared that Conneaut Lake Park would never reopen, a group called Summer Resorts, Inc., came up with a $2 million offer for the park. Their bid was accepted in May, and by July 4, Conneaut Lake Park reopened. Although the Blue Streak was not yet ready, the reopening of the park came with a renewed sense of appreciation from the area, especially since Summer Resorts eliminated the unpopular admission and parking charges.

The new owners invested heavily in the park for the 1997 season. Long-overdue infrastructure improvements were undertaken, such as new roofs and landscaping, but most importantly, the depleted ride lineup was rebuilt. The Sky Thriller looping ride, the Round Up, and the jeep-drawn tram ride that Conneaut Lake Park had sold at the 1992 auction were purchased from the now-defunct Old Indiana. Vintage Flying Scooter and Spinning Tubs rides were also acquired. Most significantly, the Blue Streak received an extensive renovation.

With the amusement park now on firm footing, Summer Resorts donated Conneaut Lake Park to the community on September 2, 1997, to be operated by a nonprofit organization, the Trustees of Conneaut Lake Park, and maintained as a community asset.

In February 1999, the trustees awarded management rights to the Conneaut Lake Park Management Group, from Youngstown, Ohio. They announced $17 million in planned improvements, including a renovation of the Hotel Conneaut, a second hotel, and a marketplace. Given the management's Youngstown connection, they also planned to draw on fond memories of Idora Park, a beloved Youngstown amusement park that closed in 1984, to expand their market. An Idora Park museum was proposed, as were plans to relocate both of Idora's roller coasters to Conneaut Lake Park.

The 1999 season got off to a promising start, with the addition of two new rides and the return of the Ultimate Trip ride after an eight-year absence. But the management company fell behind in its rental payments, and on March 27, 2000, the trustees filed to evict the group. The management company immediately filed for bankruptcy to prevent eviction, and again the future of the park was in doubt.

Conneaut Lake Park opened for the 2000 season as scheduled, and on June 28, a judge returned control to the trustees. A new spirit now prevails at Conneaut Lake Park. In 2001, the name was changed to Conneaut Lake Community Park. Advisory committees of concerned local residents have been initiated, and an organization called the Conneaut Lake Institute has been formed to develop a series of festivals. The rides will always remain a primary focus of Conneaut Lake Community Park, but it is now returning to its roots. Like the Exposition Park of old, the Conneaut Lake Community Park of the twenty-first century will be a true community gathering place.

Conneaut Lake Community Park Today

Conneaut Lake Community Park today is a throwback to the resorts of yesteryear. The lake continues to be the primary draw, with its Victorian hotel, boardwalk, beach, and Beach Club, but the nostalgic midway remains its heart. The park offers thirty-two rides, a water park, beach, Beach Club, ballroom, hotel, and a variety of other attractions.

The main entrance leads directly to Park Avenue, on which most of the major rides are situated, including the Blue Streak roller coaster, Tumble Bug, train, Flying Scooter, and bumper cars. Park Avenue is also home to the water park, with two water slides, a river ride, and a kiddie play area.

Park Avenue runs into Comstock Street, where the Convention Center, Devil's Den dark ride, and kiddieland, which features twelve kiddie rides and live ponies, are located. Along the midway, extending from the intersection of Park Avenue and Comstock Street to the lakefront, can be found food concessions and games, as well as the Dreamland Ballroom. On the lakefront are the beach, Beach Club, Hotel Conneaut, and the Commons, a large lawn that is home to most of the park's special events.

Lakemont Park

OPENED 1894

LEAP THE DIPS, THE WORLD'S OLDEST ROLLER COASTER, HAS BEEN THE heart of Lakemont Park in Altoona since 1902. It has survived through many hardships—destructive floods, neglect, and financial problems. It sat abandoned for fifteen years, escaping demolition only because its owner had more pressing needs for the money. Today at Lakemont Park, a shopping village, a minor-league baseball stadium, and an ice-skating rink surround the roller coaster and other rides. Much more than just an amusement park, Lakemont is a true community gathering place.

A Simple Trolley Park

Lakemont Park is one of the last remaining trolley parks in the United States. In 1893, the Altoona & Logan Valley Railroad purchased a 95-acre tract of land on the south side of Altoona on which to create a resort to attract evening and weekend riders. Since 1879, this formerly mined area had been used for picnicking. The trolley line was extended to the land, and in the spring of 1894, Lakemont Park opened to the public. The focal point of the new park was a 13-acre lake that had been dug in the late 1880s. Among the attractions that first season were the Gravity Road roller coaster and a carousel, both constructed by Amadius Sink, rowboats and a motor launch in the lake, a large open-air theater, a greenhouse, and elaborate floral displays throughout the grounds. Next to the lake was the park's centerpiece, the Casino, a 12,000-square-foot building used for live entertainment; civic, political, cultural, and religious events; and a shelter for ice skaters in winter.

Lakemont Park
700 Park Ave.
Altoona, PA 16602
814-949-PARK
or 800-434-8006
www.lakemontparkfun.com

The motor launch was one of Lakemont Park's original attractions. AUTHOR'S COLLECTION

Two fires caused damage in the early 1900s: the carousel was burned in 1900, and the roller coaster in 1901. In 1902, Lakemont undertook a major expansion, adding three rides. A new carousel was built by E. Joy Morris of Philadelphia, one of the state's first large-scale amusement ride builders, and featured forty-six figures, including goats, camels, giraffes, donkeys, deer, a tiger, a sea monster, and a lion. Nearby, Morris built the Leap the Dips, which, at 41 feet tall and with 1,170 feet of track, represented the latest in roller coaster technology. The ride's top speed was 10 miles per hour. The third ride added was a forerunner of today's water rides, Shoot the Chutes, an inclined plane that deposited boats into the park's lake. A donkey pulled the boats to the top of the structure.

As the golden age of the amusement park dawned in the 1920s, Lakemont Park continued to grow. A new dance hall and a bumper car building, which still stands, were built in 1923. In 1927, the park added a second roller coaster, the Twister, designed and built by the Philadelphia Toboggan Company. Located next to the Leap the Dips, the ride stood 57 feet tall and was 1,700 feet long. Unlike the milder Leap the Dips, the Twister was a high-speed thriller featuring a series of twisting drops.

The construction of the Twister represented the pinnacle of Lakemont Park's early years. But the park was soon struggling. With the increasing popularity of the automobile, other recreation areas were now within a

 **VISITING**

LAKEMONT PARK

LOCATION

Lakemont Park is located on the south side of Altoona, just off I-99 at the Frankstown Road exit (Exit 32).

OPERATING SCHEDULE

The park opens at noon on weekends in May and September, and at 11 A.M. daily from Memorial Day through the weekend before Labor Day. Closing time varies.

ADMISSION

Parking and admission to Lakemont Park are free, except for certain special events. You can pay by the ride or purchase an all-day pass for less than $10. The go-carts, games, and miniature golf cost extra.

FOOD

Lakemont Park has about ten food concessions, including the Lakeside Café, with burgers, chicken, and hot dogs; Cousin Ralph's Pizza; and stands in the Island Waterpark and in kiddieland. You may bring your own food into the park; tables are available on a first-come, first-served basis.

FOR CHILDREN

The kiddieland is located near the front entrance and features six kiddie rides, including a scaled-down roller coaster, Ferris wheel, and merry-go-round. It has its own food stand, offering hot dogs, hamburgers, and popcorn chicken.

Most of the rides in Lakemont Park can be enjoyed by the entire family, including Leap the Dips, the train, and the Pirates' Cove water play area.

SPECIAL FEATURES

Lakemont Park is one of the least expensive amusement parks in America, with an all-day pass available for under $10.

Leap the Dips is the world's oldest operating roller coaster and the last figure-eight-style roller coaster still in existence. Although its drops (9 feet) and speed (10 miles per hour) are tame by today's standards, it is a priceless throwback to a simpler time.

Skyliner, Lakemont Park's other wooden roller coaster, is one of the few wooden roller coasters to have been relocated from another amusement park.

TIME REQUIRED

Lakemont Park can be enjoyed in as little as four hours.

TOURING TIPS

The park offers a discounted evening pass.

Check the schedule of the Altoona Curve (www.altoonacurve.com) so you can watch a baseball game during your visit to the park.

day's drive, and trolley ridership was dwindling. Attendance began to fall. The popular motor launch was scrapped in 1929, and Lakemont Park began to fall into disrepair. The Depression further hurt the park, and in 1932, the Altoona & Logan Valley Railroad went into receivership.

What seemed the final blow to Lakemont Park occurred on St. Patrick's Day of 1936, when a huge flood inundated Pennsylvania and all but destroyed the park. The park's rowboats were pressed into service to rescue stranded area residents, but the park all but vanished. Ride and building foundations were washed out, the lake was filled with debris, trees were toppled, the greenhouse was destroyed, and the meandering paths through the woods were washed away.

A County Asset

Faced with its own financial problems, the Altoona & Logan Valley Railroad decided that Lakemont Park was too severely damaged by the flood to continue operating and offered the property to Blair County. Not wanting to see a valuable resource turned into a housing development, the Altoona community banded together. The community was able to secure rehabilitation funds from the Works Progress Administration (WPA), local merchants donated materials, and schoolchildren raised funds.

THE SCHUTES,   LAKEMONT PARK.

Shoot the Chutes was added in 1902. AUTHOR'S COLLECTION

The Twister operated at Lakemont Park from 1927 until it was destroyed by the 1936 flood. PHOTO BY PHILADELPHIA TOBOGGAN COMPANY

The county took control of Lakemont Park on June 18, 1937, and the community immediately went to work to restore the park, cutting fallen trees into firewood, dredging the lake, clearing away the mud, and rebuilding washed-out paths. Buildings were repaired and repainted, the playground was renovated, the Casino remodeled, and a new bandstand constructed. The Twister was too severely damaged to justify rebuilding, and the ride was torn down. Lakemont Park reopened in 1939. Its new centerpiece was a large swimming pool, constructed on an island in the lake.

Changes at the park were minimal through the 1940s. Lakemont added three kiddie rides in 1950 in response to the postwar baby boom. The trolley line ceased operation altogether in 1954. In 1957, a showboat was added on the lake. The 1923 vintage dance hall was converted into the Monster Den dark ride in 1960.

But Lakemont Park found it increasingly difficult to compete. The expanding Kennywood in Pittsburgh and Hersheypark near Harrisburg drew away visitors, and the aging park facilities and dwindling county resources made Lakemont increasingly difficult to maintain.

To obtain the funds to keep the park operating, Lakemont's eighty-year-old hand-crafted carousel and showboat were sold in 1982. This brought in $225,000, which covered the cost of a new merry-go-round with aluminum horses as well as some much-needed upgrades.

But by now, some people were starting to appreciate Lakemont Park's nostalgic atmosphere, which had been virtually unchanged since the 1890s. The Smithsonian Institution even studied the park as an excellent example of an early-twentieth-century trolley park.

In 1983, new management undertook some further renovations, and Lakemont Park enjoyed a brief resurgence. The season was a success, and the park made a profit for the first time in six years. The park continued to generate a profit in 1984, but the Blair County commissioners decided that Lakemont again had become a burden on county resources.

The Boyertown Fiasco

In 1985, Blair County received a proposal from the locally based Boyer Bros. Candy Company to transform the park into a theme park modeled after the successful Hersheypark. The commissioners, wanting to boost the local economy, saw a potential tourism boom in the Boyer proposal, but they faced opposition from some local residents who did not want county-owned land used for a profit-making venture. There were also objections to the implementation of a gate charge, thus removing public park space from the free use of county residents. As a result, a suit was filed against Blair County to stop the project, and Boyer Bros. president Anthony Forgione decided to drop his plans. But other area residents liked Forgione's idea and marched through the streets of the city and past the Boyer factory to show their support for his plan. They presented Forgione with a petition with forty thousand signatures. This changed Forgione's mind, and in September he signed a fifteen-year lease that gave him control of Lakemont Park. Forgione pledged to maintain the character of the park, telling the Altoona *Mirror,* "We're not going in with bulldozers and starting from scratch. We want to work with what's there. People love nostalgia and we're aware of that." But at the ground-breaking ceremony for the new theme park, Boyertown USA, Forgione hinted at things to come, saying, "The only thing that will remain in the park is the dirt. Everything else will be new from the ground up."

Work immediately started on the new facility. The campground was closed, the old whip ride was scrapped, and the Monster Den, the 1902 carousel building, and the roller rink were torn down. In place of the old Lakemont Park, Forgione promised that Boyertown would be a major theme park that would draw thousands of tourists into the area, giving a tremendous boost to the depressed economy. He projected that 750,000 people would visit Boyertown during its first season.

The focal point of Boyertown was this Main Street, which is now a shopping and office complex.

But Boyertown ran into problems almost immediately. When the revamped park opened on May 23, 1986, what had been a free park now charged a $12.95 admission, and visitors were not permitted to bring food into what used to be a picnic park. Those who remembered the densely wooded park saw that most of Lakemont's stately old trees had been removed during the construction. Many of the new rides and attractions, including the Skyliner roller coaster and water slides, were not yet open, and changes in safety regulations had forced the closure of Leap the Dips and the swimming pool. Attendance for the season totaled just 120,000 people.

Many doubted that Boyertown would open for the 1987 season, but just before the bank was scheduled to repossess the park, a plan was worked out. Boyertown opened with a revised admission policy: $3.95 for general admission or a pay-one-price fee of $9.95. The park hired the Dinn Corporation to complete work on the Skyliner, and several additional rides were constructed.

But the public continued to avoid Boyertown, and on September 18, after Forgione failed to make a loan payment, the park was foreclosed on by Pittsburgh National Bank. The bank did not want to be in the amusement park business and immediately began soliciting offers for the park. There were several offers, but the bank decided to auction Boyertown as a complete entity to the highest bidder.

The Skyliner was moved to Lakemont Park from New York in 1987.

On March 9, 1988, Ralph Albarano became the new owner. Albarano was the lead contractor when Boyertown was built and was owed $3.7 million of the park's $8 million in liabilities. He purchased Boyertown in hopes that he could recover some of the debt. He renamed it Lakemont Park and vowed to "retraditionalize" the park and make it an affordable family park once again.

Starting Over

Lakemont Park reopened on July 2, 1988, with a general admission of $1 or a pay-one-price fee of $6.50. Over $1.5 million had been spent on improvements, which included four rides, among them a train purchased from Heritage USA of Fort Mill, South Carolina, which was liquidated in the face of the scandal surrounding its owner, evangelist Jim Bakker. The elaborate Main Street was turned into a shopping village.

Lakemont continued to struggle, however. The much-reviled general admission fee was dropped for the 1989 season, but attendance remained flat, and a proposal to convert Main Street to an outlet mall failed.

In 1990, a local radio station, WALY, moved its office and studio to Lakemont's Main Street and became the marketing arm of the park. The park's name was changed to WALYland at Lakemont Park. The station tried to drum up business for the park and spur commercial development on surplus property, including Main Street and the old picnic grove. But this too was a failure, and the program was dropped by midseason.

In order to spur business, the pay-one-price admission was now cut to $5 on weekends and $2 on weekdays. This was well received, and Lakemont Park finished the season with an increase in attendance. A comeback had finally begun.

A new management team for the 1991 season undertook a number of improvements, adding a Mad Mouse roller coaster; the Toboggan, a roller-coaster-type ride; a new kiddieland area, Spins & Grins; and a miniature golf course themed to reflect Altoona's railroad heritage.

Lakemont Park enjoyed greater success over the next few years and gradually rebuilt the operation. In 1992, the park added Monster Motorway, a large go-cart ride; in 1993, a speedboat ride in the lake and two kiddie rides; and in 1994, the park's hundredth anniversary season, a go-cart track.

Bringing Back the Dips

In 1994, with the outlook for Lakemont brightening, the park took the opportunity to honor its past. The Lakemont Park Historical Society opened a museum in the former park office, a building that dates to just after World War I, and the Leap the Dips Preservation Society was formed to raise the $1 million needed to restore Leap the Dips, the world's oldest existing roller coaster. Thanks to the efforts of the American Coaster Enthusiasts, the neglected ride was named a National His-

The Leap the Dips remains the heart of Lakemont Park.

toric Landmark, and on May 16, 1998, restoration began. Given the historic nature of Leap the Dips, special care was taken to maintain the character of the ride.

The highest quality wood available was purchased a year in advance, so that it could properly acclimate; a steam box was built next to the ride so that the wood could be bent in the same manner as in 1902; and a master carpenter, experienced in building and restoring fine furniture, was hired to supervise the project. Leap the Dips reopened on Memorial Day 1999.

The only other structure at Lakemont Park older than Leap the Dips also underwent a significant change in 1999. Since 1988, the Casino had been a popular banquet facility, and the building was now expanded to accommodate the increasing crowds. Also that year, a $17 million minor-league baseball stadium for the Altoona Curve was built at the far end of the park, on the site of the former picnic groves. Next to the park entrance, a year-round ice-skating facility and parking garage were added.

Lakemont Park Today

Lakemont Park has been a survivor for over a hundred years, outlasting wars, economic downturns, changing travel patterns, floods, and an ill-fated conversion to a theme park. Today the park offers twenty-eight rides,

Lakemont Park today.

a water park, miniature golf course, and a variety of other attractions. Just past the main entrance are the miniature golf course and picnic area. To the right of the entrance is the kiddieland, featuring six kiddie rides, a Ferris wheel, and a merry-go-round.

Beyond lie most of the park rides, including the Mad Mouse roller coaster, the train, and the Toboggan. This area also features most of the park's games and food concessions, the arcade, the museum, and the Leap the Dips roller coaster. Nearby is the Island Waterpark, with three water slides, the Pirates' Cove water play area, and a bumper boat ride. In the far northern corner of the park are the go-cart area and the Skyliner roller coaster.

Blair County Ballpark, home of the Altoona Curve minor-league baseball team, the ice rink, and the Lakemont Village shopping and office area are also located on park property but are operated by separate parties.

Waldameer Park and Water World

OPENED 1896

IN 1945, PAUL NELSON'S PARENTS TOOK HIM TO ERIE, PENNSYLVANIA, TO visit their friends Alex and Ruth Moeller. In most cases, this would be an unremarkable event for an eleven-year-old boy, but this was different, because the Moellers owned an amusement park: Waldameer Park, overlooking Presque Isle State Park on Lake Erie. Nelson was entranced with the amusement park and soon began spending his summers at the facility helping out the Moellers. Eventually, he came to own the facility.

Waldameer Park has changed substantially since that day in 1945. While the picnic groves remain, the traditional rides have been joined by a water park. A giant Ferris wheel now towers over the lakefront, and a log flume ride douses riders where boats had peacefully floated. The park has changed, but its appeal has not.

Woods by the Sea

Waldameer Park began its life in the late 1880s as Hoffman's Grove, a popular picnic area. The thick chestnut groves provided the ideal location to escape the dirty, crowded conditions in Erie, a typical industrial city of the late 1800s. The popularity of Hoffman's Grove, a mere thirty-minute trolley ride from downtown, caught the attention of the Erie Electric Motor Company, the city's main trolley company. In 1896, the trolley company leased Hoffman's Grove and renamed the land Waldameer, German for "woods by the sea."

During Waldameer's early years, the park consisted of two areas. At the top of the slope, 70

**Waldameer Park
and Water World**

P.O. Box 8308
Erie, PA 16505

814-838-3591

www.waldameer.com

feet above Lake Erie, was a 10-acre picnic grove with swings, hammocks, and athletic fields. But most of the activity was concentrated on the beach at the bottom of the slope. Linked to the picnic grove by a 1,000-foot-long boardwalk, the beach area featured a swimming pool, a 110-foot-long bathhouse, a pier, a water slide, canoes, and rowboats.

Waldameer's first carousel was installed in 1902. It was replaced in 1905. The new machine featured a menagerie of animals carved by several different manufacturers, including Dentzel, Muller, and Stein & Goldstein, and it was assembled by T. M. Harton of Pittsburgh. The carousel was placed in a $7,500 building that now houses Waldameer's current merry-go-round. In 1907, Harton built Waldameer's first roller coaster, Dip the Dips, a gentle figure-eight-style ride. Expansion continued in 1909, with the addition of a 2,000-seat vaudeville theater and the Scenic Railway roller coaster. During the early years, Waldameer was almost entirely self-sufficient. A gas well was dug on property to provide backup electrical power, and water from a spring was stored in a 20,000-gallon reservoir for use in the park.

Throughout the first decade of the century, thousands traveled by streetcar to enjoy Waldameer's beach, boardwalk, and bathhouse. Patrons used an incline railway, called the Toonerville Trolley, to travel from the main portion of the park at the top of the slope down to the beach attractions. Other early attractions included the House of Hilarity fun house, also built by T. M. Harton, and a circle swing.

This cable car ride connected Waldameer Park's picnic grove with the beach in the early years. AUTHOR'S COLLECTION

Dip the Dips was Waldameer's first roller coaster, operating from 1907 to 1937.
AUTHOR'S COLLECTION

Waldameer Park replaced its original Scenic Railway in 1915 with a new $30,000 version. In 1919, because of Prohibition, the park was forced to close one of its most popular early attractions—the Hofbrau German Beer Garden, complete with singing waiters.

As the amusement park industry entered its golden age in the 1920s, George Sinclair, who owned Meyer's Lake Park in Canton, Ohio, came to Waldameer Park and built the park's largest roller coaster, the Ravine Flyer. Opened in 1922, the Ravine Flyer made use of the park's topography to create drops of up to 80 feet, and it traveled over the road that ran in front of the park. Sinclair was a major concessionaire at Waldameer during the 1920s, also building the Old Mill, a peaceful boat ride through a long tunnel.

Alex Moeller, a former German sailor, became general manager of the park during the 1920s and continued the park's expansion. In 1924, Moeller added a whip, swing ride, and train. Other rides at this time were a Caterpillar; the Dodgem; Custer Cars, an early version of today's turnpike rides; and Bluebeard's Castle, a fun house. Also during this decade, the carousel was relocated to a new building in order to spread out the park. This proved to be unsuccessful, however, and the ride was moved back to its original building after a few seasons. The new building was converted to a picnic pavilion, which is still in use.

LOCATION

Waldameer Park and Water World is located on the west side of Erie on Peninsula Drive (PA Route 832), just outside the entrance to Presque Isle State Park. From the west, exit I-90 at PA Route 832 North (Exit 18) and take it eight miles directly to the park. From the south, take I-79 to 12th Street (PA Route 5, Exit 183B). Take 12th Street two miles east to Peninsula Drive (PA Route 832) and turn left. From the east, take I-90 to I-79 North.

OPERATING SCHEDULE

The park is open weekends in May, starting on Mother's Day weekend, and Tuesday through Sunday from Memorial Day weekend through Labor Day.

Water World opens at 11 A.M., and the amusement park opens at 1 P.M. Closing times vary depending on the time of year.

ADMISSION

Admission and parking are free. Visitors can purchase an all-day ride pass or Water World pass for under $15, or a combo pass for under $20. Discounts are available for those less than 42 inches tall, and individual ride tickets are available.

FOOD

There are eleven food stands at Waldameer Park and Water World, with two located in Water World. The main food stand is in the heart of the park, near the Thunder River flume ride, and offers hot dogs, burgers, chicken, pizza, and meatball subs. You may bring your own food into the park. Tables and grills are available on a first-come, first-served basis.

FOR CHILDREN

Most of Waldameer Park's nine kiddie rides are located in the center of the park, near the Ferris wheel. In addition to the Ravine Flyer III kiddie coaster, most kids can also enjoy the Comet roller coaster. There are also several child-oriented activities in Water World, including five scaled-down water slides.

Rides for the entire family include the Ferris wheel, train, and merry-go-round. Imagination Station, next to the merry-go-round, has a variety of craft activities, such as face painting, sand art, and spin art.

SPECIAL FEATURES

Waldameer Park and Water World is an amusement park in the traditional sense, where a family can still show up with a picnic and have a full day's outing for only a few dollars.

For a park of its size, Waldameer Park and Water World has one of the best attraction lineups around. Few amusement parks can match its diversity.

(continued on page 108)

VISITING (continued from page 107)

TIME REQUIRED

A visit to both the water park and amusement park is easily a full day's outing, although the amusement park can be experienced in as little as four hours.

TOURING TIPS

Water World opens at 11 A.M., two hours earlier than the amusement park. Show up early and visit the water park first, enjoy a picnic lunch, and then enjoy the activities in the amusement park.

Presque Isle State Park is right next door to Waldameer Park and Water World. The 3,200-acre park features a wide variety of recreational activities. For more information, visit the website www.presqueisle.org.

To boost attendance during the Depression, talking movies, a relatively new phenomenon, were offered. With the repeal of Prohibition in 1933, the popular beer garden was brought back. In 1937, the aging Dip the Dips roller coaster was removed, and the dance hall burnt down. Without enough funds to rebuild the dance hall, Waldameer built an outdoor dance floor for the 1938 season, but due to the unpredictability of the weather, it met with limited success.

In August 1938, a tragedy occurred when the Ravine Flyer got caught between dips. A man rose to try to calm his hysterical sister, lost his balance, and fell 30 feet to his death. Ruth Moeller was so upset by the tragedy that her husband immediately removed the ride. The station was converted into a picnic pavilion.

As the thirties ended, the economy improved, and Waldameer once again began expanding. The first priority was to build a new dance hall; Rainbow Gardens opened in 1940.

Another tragedy struck in 1941, when a fire destroyed the Hofbrau German restaurant while a dinner for fifteen hundred was under way. Everyone was safely evacuated, but eleven people were injured, and a waitress perished when she went back inside to retrieve her coat.

World War II limited Waldameer's expansion, but the park held benefit days for the Army-Navy relief fund. In response to the national mood, several rides were given patriotic names and paint jobs. By the end of the war in 1945, Waldameer's rides included airplane swings, the Fun in the Dark dark ride, Loop-O-Plane, Tumble Bug, Flying Scooter, a miniature train, and two kiddie rides. That year, Alex Moeller, who had been leasing the grounds since the 1920s, became the owner of the park. He added a Streamliner train from the National Amusement Devices Company in 1947.

As Waldameer Park entered the 1950s, the park continued to expand. The year 1951 saw the addition of the Comet, the first roller coaster to operate at Waldameer Park since the Ravine Flyer was demolished in 1938. The Comet is a junior-size wooden roller coaster standing 45 feet tall, with a 1,400-foot-long track length and a circular loading station.

The Modern Era

Waldameer entered a quiet period over the next ten years. Ride expansion was limited, although a Flying Coaster ride was added in 1962 and the Rainbow Gardens was remodeled in 1963. In 1965, Alex Moeller died, and Paul Nelson, who had been adopted by the Moellers and had worked his way up to general manager, took over management. He immediately began to upgrade the park's aging infrastructure. Throughout the late 1960s, all-steel game buildings were constructed, ravines in the park were filled in to increase usable acreage by one-third, electrical lines were buried, and new trees were planted.

With the park modernized, Waldameer added new rides throughout the 1970s, starting with the Wacky Shack, a large, two-story dark ride designed by William Tracy, one of the all-time great dark ride creators. The popularity of the Wacky Shack prompted Waldameer to have Tracy build the Pirate's Cove, a large, walk-through attraction, in 1972. Also added that year was a new miniature train named the L. Ruth Express,

The Comet has been thrilling visitors since 1951.

The Wacky Shack dark ride joined the ride lineup in 1970.

after Alex Moeller's widow. In 1978, Paul Nelson assumed full ownership of the park. That year, patrons were greeted by a new sky ride manufactured by O. D. Hopkins of New Hampshire.

Expansion slowed in the early 1980s, although a kiddie ride was added in 1983 and bumper boats were added in 1984. By 1985, Waldameer was a successful local amusement park with a well-balanced ride lineup. But, deciding that the park had reached a plateau, Nelson embarked on a major expansion and renovation program.

With the water park craze sweeping America, it was decided that a full-scale water park should be the first phase in the expansion, and Water World made its debut for the 1986 season. Initially it was a modest operation, with two water slides and several activity pools. But that would soon change.

With the demand for antique carousel horses peaking in the late 1980s, Waldameer auctioned off its eighty-three-year-old carousel and antique Blue Goose kiddie ride, receiving over $1 million. A portion of the proceeds was used to restore the old carousel building and purchase a new merry-go-round with sixty horses that moved up and down, unlike the original. But most of the funds were put into expanding the increasingly popular water park. A complex of five new water slides was built in 1989, followed in the early 1990s by the Bermuda Triangle, a complex of three tube slides originating from one 47-foot-tall tower. By now, Water World was one of the largest water parks in Pennsylvania, and Waldameer was drawing larger and larger crowds.

In 1992, Nelson introduced a ten-year expansion plan that would transform the park still further. A play area for kids and the Sea Dragon swinging ship were added that year. In 1994, a giant Ferris wheel was built above the bumper boat pond. Placed on a high platform, the 100-foot-tall wheel stood nearly 180 feet above the lake, providing a spectacular view of Lake Erie and the nearby Presque Isle peninsula.

The park celebrated its hundredth anniversary in 1996 with its most ambitious project yet, the Thunder River log flume. It replaced the Old Mill ride and featured a 1,300-foot-long trough, a storm tunnel, and two splash-down hills.

Waldameer Park closed out the twentieth century by adding three new rides in 1999—Ali Baba, a huge flying carpet; and two kiddie rides, the Frog Hopper and the Convoy. In 2000, a kiddie roller coaster, the Ravine Flyer III, replaced the bumper boats. While this addition pleased Waldameer's smallest thrill seekers, the park's bigger ones are eagerly awaiting the future opening of the Ravine Flyer II, a large wooden roller

Waldameer purchased this carousel after the original was sold in 1988.

The addition of Water World kicked a new era of growth that continues to this day.

coaster named after the park's earlier ride. Like its predecessor, Ravine Flyer II will cross over Peninsula Drive and take advantage of the lakefront slope to enhance the experience. Although it will stand only 78 feet high, the largest drop will plunge 121 feet and the track will cross over itself eight times.

Waldameer Park Today

Waldameer Park and Water World today features twenty-four rides, including nine for kids, as well as a water park, and picnic groves. The park has three entrances, two leading into the picnic grove and a third located near the Thunder River log flume and Rainbow Gardens ballroom.

The large, wooded picnic grove leads directly into the main midway, where most of the rides and concessions are located, including the merry-go-round, Comet roller coaster, and bumper cars. At the end of the midway, several larger rides, including the Giant Wheel, Sea Dragon, Sky Ride, Wacky Shack dark ride, Thunder River flume, and Pirate's Cove fun house, surround most of the kiddie rides.

The entrance to Water World is located next to the Comet roller coaster, off the main midway. Water World offers eleven water slides, a river ride, a pool, five kiddie water slides, and three kiddie pools.

Kennywood

OPENED 1898

THE HISTORY OF PITTSBURGH CAN BE TRACED ALONG THE MONONGAHELA River. At the river's end, where it merges with the Allegheny River to form the Ohio River, the Monongahela passes the former site of Fort Duquesne, where Pittsburgh was founded as a frontier outpost in the mid-1700s. Upriver, former steel mill sites are being redeveloped into campuses for technology companies, and urban neighborhoods are seeing new life as homes to artists and young professionals. Along the river about 10 miles from downtown Pittsburgh is one of Pittsburgh's most enduring institutions: Kennywood, the last remaining example of what used to be the cornerstone of the American amusement park industry— the large urban amusement park.

While in most cities such parks have been supplanted by corporate mega theme parks, Kennywood continues to thrive. Although it is home to modern thrillers, such as the 251-foot-tall Pitt Fall and Phantom's Revenge, one of the world's fastest roller coasters, Kennywood continues to cherish its past and is home to an extensive array of vintage amusement park rides that are as popular as ever. It is this respect for their history that has made Kennywood one of only two operating amusement parks to be listed as a National Historic Landmark, and the only one to earn a National Trust for Historic Preservation Honor Award.

A New Playground

In the late 1800s, trolley companies in Pittsburgh were competing for business, and most of them built their own amusement parks to generate traffic on the weekend. By 1906, nearly two

Kennywood
4800 Kennywood Blvd.
West Mifflin, PA 15102
412-461-0500
www.kennywood.com

One of Kennywood's first rides, the Old Mill, has been entertaining visitors to Kennywood since 1901. AUTHOR'S COLLECTION

dozen different trolley parks were operating in southwestern Pennsylvania. One such company was the Monongahela Traction Company, which ran from Pittsburgh's Oakland neighborhood to the city of Duquesne. Controlled by one of Pittsburgh's best-known industrial families, the Mellons, the line found the perfect piece of property for such a place in a 150-acre tract midway between the mill towns of Homestead and Duquesne. The land, owned by Anthony Kenny, had long been a popular picnic ground with locals, who called it Kenny's Woods. Given that these amusement parks were such a new concept, the trolley company leased the land from the Kenny family rather than purchasing it outright.

The March 1898 *Street Railway Review* reported on the company's plans to create a "first class summer resort," called Kennywood, with attractions such as a summer theater, a dancing pavilion, bowling alleys, a bandstand, a dining hall, a baseball diamond, boating, and tennis courts.

The park was open to visitors that first season, yet Kennywood was still a work in progress, and most attractions did not open until 1899. The Kennywood of those early years was much more sedate than today's action-packed parks, but it was beginning to feature many of the attractions that remain beloved landmarks. The boating lake was the centerpiece of Kennywood when it opened for the first time on Decoration

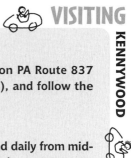

LOCATION

Kennywood is located 10 miles from downtown Pittsburgh, on PA Route 837 along the Monongahela River. Take I-376 to Swissvale (Exit 7), and follow the arrows to Kennywood.

OPERATING SCHEDULE

Kennywood is open selected weekends starting in mid-April, and daily from mid-May through Labor Day. Gates open at 10:30 A.M., and rides begin to open at 11 A.M. The park closes at about 10 P.M. The week before Labor Day, the park does not open until 5 P.M. weekdays.

ADMISSION

You can purchase a Ride-All-Day pass for under $30 or a general admission pass for under $10 plus individual ride tickets. Adult rides require one to four tickets; kiddieland rides require one ticket. General admission tickets may be purchased only by guests over twenty-one or those subject to Kennywood's ride limitations due to height or physical restrictions. Ride-All-Day passes provide unlimited access to all rides and attractions, with the exception of the Skycoaster, paddle boats, miniature golf, and games, which cost extra.

FOOD

Kennywood features about thirty food concessions, ranging from popcorn and cotton candy carts to the Parkside Terrace, a cafeteria with a wide array of hearty, home-style meals, including turkey, roast beef, fried shrimp, pasta, and sandwiches. Try to get a seat on the large, covered porch for the best people watching in the park. The Carousel Court has covered seating and three separate food stands.

Other notable stands include the Pagoda with its hot sausage sandwiches; the Lucky with its corn dogs and funnel cakes; the Pizza Warehouse and West View Pizza Pavilion with pizza and sandwiches; and the Golden Nugget and Big Dipper for ice cream. Don't miss the Potato Patch, serving up Kennywood's world-famous fresh-cut french fries.

Kennywood is known as a picnic park, and you may bring your own food. Tables are available on a first-come, first-served basis.

FOR CHILDREN

Kennywood features a self-contained kiddieland, with thirteen rides and several child-oriented games. Favorites include the Cadillac Cars, roller coaster, and merry-go-round. Nearby are a number of family-oriented rides, including the Auto Race, train, carousel, and Log Jammer. Garfield, Odie, and Kenny Kangaroo, Kennywood's official mascots, make appearances throughout the park during the day.

(continued on page 116)

VISITING (continued from page 115)

KENNYWOOD

SPECIAL FEATURES

In many ways, Kennywood is a living museum of the history of amusement parks. The park is full of vintage buildings, such as those housing the Parkside Terrace and Carousel Court, along with a wide array of lovingly maintained antique rides, including the Old Mill, whip, Turtle, Auto Race, Noah's Ark, and carousel, all of which are as popular as ever. The park is full of historical markers telling the history of various rides and buildings.

At the same time, Kennywood is renowned for its six roller coasters: the Jack Rabbit, one of the oldest operating roller coasters in the world, with its famous double dip; the Racer, the last continuous-track racing roller coaster in America; the Thunderbolt, one of the top-ranked roller coasters in the world; Phantom's Revenge, one of the world's tallest and fastest; the Exterminator, a heavily themed indoor roller coaster; and Lil' Phantom, for the kids.

Lost Kennywood is a tribute to the old-fashioned amusement park. Like many amusement parks in the early part of the twentieth century, the centerpiece is the splash-down pond for the Pittsburg Plunge. Surrounding the pond are several buildings patterned after structures that existed at amusement parks in the early part of the twentieth century. Thousands of white lights adorn the rides and buildings, so don't miss it at night.

TIME REQUIRED

Kennywood is a full-day outing. If your time is limited, the larger rides can be enjoyed in about six hours.

TOURING TIPS

Arrive when the gates open at 10:30 A.M. If you bring a picnic, get a table and then head for Lost Kennywood, as crowds tend to reach this part of the park last. Try to hit most of the larger rides early in the day or after 8 P.M., as lines tend to be shorter during these times.

Ride-All-Day passes are discounted during the week.

(Memorial) Day in 1898. Long since a popular venue for circus acts, the lake offered rowboats and a walking path along its edge.

Kennywood's dance hall and its first ride, a merry-go-round from Gustav Dentzel of Philadelphia, appeared in 1899. The carousel was placed in a substantial new building that is now the Carousel Court food service area. That same year, one of Kennywood's most enduring traditions was born: Nationality Day, when many of Pittsburgh's ethnic groups converge on Kennywood for special food, entertainment, and cultural traditions. The first Nationality Day occurred when a large group of Scottish clans gathered at the park to share cultural traditions. Today nearly a dozen ethnic groups gather at Kennywood every year to celebrate their heritage.

The Casino Restaurant, now the Parkside Terrace cafeteria, opened in 1900. Also added that year were a ball field and a bandstand. As the new century dawned, an increasingly sophisticated public began to demand larger and more elaborate rides. In response, Kennywood added the Old Mill in 1901, today the park's oldest operating ride. A 1902 promotional brochure described the new ride as "a delightful ride on the water, through dark caverns and deep caves brightened here and there by bright flashes of light, showing grotesque and fascinating scenes. A most novel and realistic form of entertainment."

Kennywood began to earn the title of "Coaster Capital of the World" in 1902, with the opening of the park's first roller coaster, the Figure Eight. Built by Fred Ingersoll of Pittsburgh, the leading roller coaster manufacturer of his era, the ride was located at the front entrance where the Turnpike now stands.

Other rides followed in quick succession. The Steeplechase, on which riders traveled on mechanical horses on a half-mile-long roller-coaster-type track, was added in 1903. Another roller coaster, the Scenic Railway, started entertaining visitors in 1905.

But while the park was growing, its owner, now known as the Pittsburgh Railways Company, wanted to get out of the amusement park business. In 1906, it sold the park to Kennywood Park Limited, a partnership of A. S. McSwigan, F. W. Henninger, and A. F. Meghan, among the most experienced park operators in western Pennsylvania. It was the last change in ownership that Kennywood would see.

From the beginning, the new owners insisted that they would run a high-class operation forbidding "alcohol, gambling and disorder." They also knew that to attract patrons to the park, they would have to continually invest in operations. Management continues to embrace both policies. During the new owners' first few seasons, the emphasis was on upgrading existing operations. Expansion began in earnest in 1910, with the addition of the first Racer, a $50,000 roller coaster built by Fred Ingersoll on the current site of Kiddieland.

Another roller coaster, the Speed-O-Plane, Kennywood's first high-speed roller coaster, replaced the Scenic Railway in 1911. That year, Kennywood also suffered its first major fire, which destroyed the motion picture theater, penny arcade, and shooting gallery. The park was unfazed by the fire, however, and expansion continued in 1913 with a new carousel, carved by T. M. Harton, owner of nearby West View Park. Unlike the original carousel, this was a state-of-the-art machine that featured animals that moved up and down.

Aerial view of Kennywood from around World War I. AUTHOR'S COLLECTION

Good Times and Bad

The Roaring Twenties was an era of great prosperity and innovation for the amusement park industry, and the first ride Kennywood added that decade took advantage of this. The Jack Rabbit, a roller coaster opened in 1921, was built by John Miller, the most prolific roller coaster designer in history. It utilized a then-new technique to lock the train to the tracks, allowing for higher speeds and bigger hills. The 2,132-foot-long ride's most unusual feature is a double dip that drops into one of Kennywood's ravines and lifts riders out of their seats. The Jack Rabbit remains a favorite and is the world's seventh-oldest operating roller coaster.

In 1924, Kennywood decided that their youngest guests needed a special place to call their own. The park became an industry trendsetter by opening one of the first kiddielands at any amusement park. Located near the Jack Rabbit, it featured four kid-size rides. One, the Ferris wheel, is still in operation. Also that year, John Miller built another roller coaster, the Pippin, in a ravine across the park from the Jack Rabbit.

Expansion continued in 1925 with the opening of a swimming pool, located on the current site of Lost Kennywood. The pool was a dominant feature until it closed in 1973. Another famous Kennywood tradition also started that year, when the now-famous yellow directional arrows began appearing on the region's roadways.

Although the park had grown tremendously over the previous several years, it was 1927 that truly established Kennywood as one of America's major amusement parks. Kiddieland was moved to its current location and expanded from four to eight rides, and some of the park's most enduring and beloved rides made their debuts. John Miller returned to construct his third roller coaster at Kennywood—the current Racer. It replaced the park's original Racer and is 73 feet tall and 2,250 feet long. It is the last remaining continuous-track racing roller coaster in the country. While it appears to be a double-track ride, it actually has a single track, and trains leaving from the right-hand side of the station return on the left-hand side, and vice versa.

Other new rides were also added in 1927. A new larger whip replaced the one added in 1918, and the Turtle was purchased from Traver Engineering of nearby Beaver Falls, Pennsylvania, at the time the largest amusement ride manufacturer in the world. Both rides remain favorites. But probably the most spectacular addition that season was a new carousel. The immense ride features sixty-four hand-carved horses, a lion, a tiger, four chariots, and fourteen hundred lights. William Dentzel, son of Gustav, the carver of Kennywood's first carousel, manufactured it for the Philadelphia Sesquicentennial Exposition of 1926. Manufacturing delays meant that the ride was not ready to debut at the fair, and as a result, it was offered to Kennywood. The park purchased it for $25,000 but discovered that, at 54 feet in diameter, it was too big for the existing carousel building. As a result, it was placed in a new, $10,000 steel building next to the old carousel pavilion, which was converted into a food service facility.

As the 1930s dawned, the Depression was causing hundreds of amusement parks around the country to shut down. Kennywood added a new Auto Race ride in 1930, in which miniature electrically powered race cars zoom around a wooden track, but the business strategy soon switched from expansion to survival. As a result, the park relied on promotions and low-cost activities to attract longtime customers. Kennywood offered a free playground, a Wild West show, free stage acts, ballroom dancing, and Mouse City, a miniature city containing three hundred white mice.

By the mid-1930s, the economy was slowly improving, and Kennywood resumed expansion. The park added a new junior-size roller coaster, the Teddy Bear, in 1935, and Noah's Ark, one of Kennywood's most enduring symbols, in 1936. Built at a cost of $20,000, Noah's Ark is a large, rocking boat sitting on top of Mount Ararat, in which guests encounter a variety of obstacles as they venture through the attraction. Other rides were soon added, but almost as soon as the economic recovery was complete, America entered World War II. Growth at Kennywood ground to a halt as attention shifted to supporting the war effort.

But as the war was winding down in 1945, Kennywood was able to add a miniature train that originally operated at the 1939 New York World's Fair. It still travels along the bluff high above the Monongahela River, and today provides a ride through displays of local history. Kennywood capped off the 1940s by expanding into a new midway area next to the train ride. Anchoring this area was the Little Dipper, a new junior roller coaster that replaced the Teddy Bear in 1948. Built by the park, the Little Dipper stood 40 feet tall and was originally 1,250 feet long. In 1951, an additional 400 feet of track was added so that two trains could be operated simultaneously.

Adapting to a Changing World

As the 1950s dawned, Kennywood found itself confronting a changing world. In 1950, television first came to Pittsburgh. Kennywood immediately began advertising on the new medium and was soon promoting appearances by television personalities. Cast members from the TV show "Howdy Doody" were regular attractions, and a 1957 appearance by the Lone Ranger attracted forty-five thousand fans. The park also kicked off the decade by starting a new tradition, meant to stimulate traffic in the slow late-summer period: the annual Fall Fantasy Parade, featuring floats and marching bands. But while new traditions were started, others came to an end. In the face of changing tastes, Kennywood turned the dance pavilion into the Enchanted Forest fun house in 1952.

Noah's Ark, added in 1936, is one of Kennywood's most enduring symbols.

The Dipper entertained Kennywood's younger guests from 1948 until 1984.

In response to the postwar baby boom, Kennywood spent much of the decade expanding Kiddieland, adding such classics as the Sky Fighter in 1950, the Hand Cars in 1953, the kiddie Turnpike in 1955, and the Helicopters in 1958. In 1955, Kennywood's first European-made ride, the Rotor, made its debut. It created such a sensation that patrons were charged admission just to watch the riders defy gravity in the spinning drum.

Kennywood's first steel-track roller coaster, the Wild Mouse, made its debut in 1958. Built by B. A. Schiff of Miami, the roller coaster relied on sharp turns rather than steep drops for its thrills. That same year also marked the end of an era, as trolley service to the park ended. Patrons now had to get to the park by car or bus.

In 1964, Carl Henninger took over as chairman. At the time, permanent improvements were still considered a risky proposition, as Kennywood continued to lease the property from the Kenny family, and the lease required any permanent attractions to be left behind should Kennywood be evicted. But Henninger felt that with the growing influence of theme parks, Kennywood had to add larger rides to remain competitive.

As a result, in 1966, the park replaced its aging Laff in the Dark ride, built in 1930, with the Turnpike. Costing over $100,000, the miniature car ride was a copy of Disney's popular Autopia ride and represented the park's most expensive addition to that point. The following season, the old dance pavilion was again converted, this time to the Ghost Ship,

Kennywood's largest dark ride ever. For the 1968 season, in response to the flashy new rides being added at the huge corporate-owned theme parks, management decided that the park needed a new roller coaster.

Current chairman Carl Hughes recalls how difficult it was to find a location for the new roller coaster at the tightly packed park. "Carl Henninger tried to figure out a way to add a roller coaster and asked renowned roller coaster designer John Allen for assistance. We even talked about tearing down the Racer and building something there. Then he had the idea of putting in an out-and-back-style roller coaster along the bluff. But that would have meant removing several rides, and Allen said there still wouldn't be enough room."

Finally, Henninger and the park's head mechanic arrived at the idea of rebuilding the middle of the Pippin. Kennywood retained the start and end of the ride, which plunged into the ravine, added a series of twisting drops, and the Thunderbolt was born. Because of its use of the ravine, the 2,900-foot-long ride's largest drop (95 feet) does not occur until the end of the ride, and the train is not hauled to the top of the chain lift until it has plunged into the ravine twice.

Kennywood entered a whole new era in 1972, when it was finally able to purchase the land from the Kenny family. With the threat of eviction

The now legendary Thunderbolt was built in 1968, a time when few parks were adding roller coasters.

Kennywood's Racer— There's No Other Ride Like It

With its graceful wooden arches in a loading station adorned with classic incandescent lights, a sign that twinkles at night, and a section of track that rumbles over the station roof, it's not hard to see that Kennywood's Racer is a one-of-a-kind roller coaster.

The Racer's most distinctive feature is its twin-track layout. Few roller coasters in the country allow two trains to travel side-by-side, with riders competing to see which is the fastest. When the Racer was built in 1927, it was common practice to construct racing roller coasters as one continuous loop, rather than as two separate tracks, as is common today. Called a *reverse curve*, this unique feature means that riders who leave the station on the right-hand track return on the left-hand track, and vice versa. It also means that if you ride the Racer only once, you have experienced only half the ride.

The Racer is 72 feet high, has a maximum drop of 50 feet, and features 2,250 feet of track. The Racer's station was restored to its original appearance in 1990, reversing a 1960 "modernization."

In addition to being a unique ride, the Racer is a true piece of amusement park history. The ride was built by John Miller, the most prolific roller coaster builder in history, and was done during the golden age of roller coasters, when amusement parks around the world were competing to build exciting rides. It was one of the first rides to feature one-stop loading. Older roller coasters typically stopped twice: first to unload riders, and a second time to load new ones. A single stop to unload and load riders at the same time resulted in shorter lines. Most modern roller coasters use this feature.

no longer guiding their business decisions, their way of doing business changed. "We could build without impunity," says Hughes.

Kennywood's first big attraction after gaining control of the land was the addition of the Log Jammer in 1975, its first million-dollar ride. Built by Arrow Dynamics, the leading log flume manufacturer of the 1970s, the 1,600-foot-long flume features a 27-foot roller-coaster-style drop and a 53-foot-tall final plunge. The Log Jammer represented an important investment for Kennywood in that it showed that the park had the resources to compete with the big theme parks. Soon any talk of a new theme park opening in Pittsburgh to steal business from Kennywood was silenced.

While the opening of the Log Jammer represented a high point in Kennywood's history, a low point also occurred that season, when the biggest fire ever hit the park. The fire destroyed the Ghost Ship dark ride, two kiddie rides, and the Round Up ride. But the rest of the park never closed during the fire. The affected area was roped off, and it was business as usual in the rest of Kennywood. As soon as the ashes cooled, the debris was cleared and new rides were built.

In 1977, a new midway area was added behind Noah's Ark. This area became home to some of the industry's newest rides, such as the Enterprise, one of a new generation of high-speed thrill rides that were increasingly found in the industry.

By the 1980s, Kennywood was able to compete with the big theme parks. The park added flashy new rides on a regular basis: the Laser Loop, Kennywood's first looping roller coaster, in 1980; the Gold Rusher in 1981; the Pirate Ship in 1982; the Wave Swinger in 1984; the Raging Rapids, which replaced the bandstand and Little Dipper, in 1985; and the Wonder Wheel, a giant Ferris wheel adorned with thousands of colorful lights, in 1986.

While Kennywood's future now seemed secure, it faced new challenges as the economy of Pittsburgh underwent radical change. The steel mills that had been the park's neighbors since the beginning were shutting down, and the mill workers that provided such a large part of the park's business were disappearing. Kennywood estimated that the loss of the industrial picnics cost the park 150,000 visitors annually. Though this was too much for parks in other cities, Kennywood pressed forward and worked to lure workers in Pittsburgh's new economy. Soon the expansive picnic groves that had accommodated generations of mill workers were filled with bankers, computer programmers, and healthcare personnel.

A National Treasure

By the end of the 1980s, America was beginning to realize that Kennywood's strategy of investment in new attractions, combined with impeccable care of beloved classics, had created a living history of the American amusement park industry. Although the latest million-dollar rides attracted the most attention, the park still featured the same tree-shaded Victorian atmosphere it had from the beginning. It was the type of amusement park that had all but disappeared from the rest of America in the era of takeovers, downsizing, and disposable products. Because Kennywood had become such a special place, it was named a National Historic Landmark in 1987, one of only two operating amusement parks to be honored in this manner.

The 1990s can best be remembered as the decade in which Kennywood evolved from a beloved local institution into a nationally known park. It was thrust into the spotlight in 1991, when the Steel Phantom first sent riders through its twisting track. Seeking a major new attraction to replace the aging Laser Loop and compete with larger parks, Kennywood started evaluating designs for a major steel roller coaster that would take advantage of its ravines to produce a truly notable ride. As Kennywood was evaluating different designs, the park realized that it could add another 10 feet to the proposed ride's largest hill and have a drop longer than that of any roller coaster on the planet. It would also be the world's fastest. The result was a truly groundbreaking ride. From its first drop of 160 feet, the coaster plunged over the side of a hill down a 225-foot drop through the Thunderbolt's structure, reaching speeds of 85 miles per hour before turning riders upside down four times. The ride attracted coaster enthusiasts from around the world, who discovered something that locals had known for generations—Kennywood was a unique place with a special personality.

While the Steel Phantom attracted most of the attention, Kennywood also spent the decade maintaining its historic treasures and restoring classic rides and buildings, including the Racer, the Old Mill, the Auto Race, the Casino, and the original carousel pavilion. In 1996, the park undertook a $1 million rebuilding of Noah's Ark, restoring the original boat and rebuilding Mount Ararat.

The increased attendance from the Steel Phantom and Kennywood's appreciation of its heritage led to the park's opening in 1995 of its largest investment ever—Lost Kennywood. Needing additional land for expan-

The Racer's facade was restored to its original appearance in 1990.

The record-breaking Steel Phantom became a landmark in 1991. Its first two hills were retained when Phantom's Revenge was constructed in 2001.

The entrance to Lost Kennywood is a one-third-scale replica of the front entrance of Pittsburgh's Luna Park.

sion, park management started to develop a multiphase replacement of one of its parking lots. While it was originally proposed to add a restroom building, a dark ride, and some concessions as a first phase, the project soon evolved into a major area that would be the first themed tribute to the history of the American amusement park. The industry had never seen anything like Lost Kennywood. Patterned after Pittsburgh's Luna Park, one of Kennywood's long-gone competitors, the area features an array of fanciful buildings arranged around a lagoon. With all of the rides and buildings adorned with thousands of electric lights, it is a spectacular scene at night. The new area is anchored by the Pittsburg Plunge, a large water ride, and also includes a relocated whip and other rides.

As Kennywood has matured, it has become increasingly difficult to find areas in which to expand. Because of this, two of the park's most recent attractions have grown upward instead of outward. In 1994, Kennywood was the first amusement park to add a Skycoaster, a 200-foot-tall A-frame under which riders are suspended by a cable. The cable is hauled back to a second tower, then the riders pull a ripcord and free-fall at speeds up to 70 miles per hour in a giant swinging motion. Erected over the lake, the Skycoaster created a huge sensation, and it is now an industry staple.

Kennywood reached new heights in 1997 with the addition of the 251-foot-tall Pitt Fall, at the time the world's tallest free-fall attraction. With the park reaching maximum density in 1999, Kennywood expanded outside its original boundaries for the first time in building the Exterminator.

This ride continued Kennywood's tradition of creating unique roller coasters by enclosing a 1,500-foot-long, 50-foot-tall Wild Mouse–style roller coaster in a large building. As riders venture through a subterranean world in rat-shaped vehicles, they are chased through the ride by exterminators.

One of Kennywood's greatest challenges has been to make room for new attractions. In 2000, the Wonder Wheel gave way to the Aero 360, a large, modern thriller that flips riders upside down, while another major change was announced. Although the Steel Phantom was still a favorite of coaster fans, the space-constrained park decided to replace it with a new roller coaster. After the announcement was made in March 2000, the Steel Phantom's most ardent fans set up websites and sent the park letters imploring Kennywood to reconsider the decision. As a result, the park decided to compromise and retain Steel Phantom's most exciting features—the two large drops that kick off the ride—lengthening the biggest drop to 230 feet and adding a third hill, 120 feet tall, a tunnel under the Thunderbolt, and several high-speed hills.

The new roller coaster, Phantom's Revenge, embodies everything that Kennywood stands for: While park management is not afraid to move forward and add the latest in new amusement park attractions, it maintains a respect for its heritage.

Kennywood Today

Today's Kennywood is a delightful mix of old and new. Century-old trees tower above intricate landscaping and an eclectic collection of buildings. Lovingly maintained antique rides stand shoulder-to-shoulder with modern thrillers, and visitors still haul baskets and coolers into the picnic groves.

Kennywood features forty-five rides, including thirteen for kids. The main entrance leads through a tunnel underneath Kennywood Boulevard to the entrance area. Found here are the Old Mill, the Turnpike, and one of the two picnic groves. This midway leads to Kennywood's lake, which is surrounded by the Jack Rabbit and Racer roller coasters, Log Jammer, Skycoaster, and Aero 360. Also in this area are the kiddieland, the carousel, and the second picnic area.

Beyond the lake are the Thunderbolt, Noah's Ark, Turtle, and many of Kennywood's newer rides, including the Raging Rapids, Enterprise, Pirate, Wipeout, and Phantom's Revenge. Lost Kennywood is located beyond Phantom's Revenge and is home to the Pittsburg Plunge water ride, whip, Exterminator, and Pitt Fall.

Live shows take place at the Garden Stage in the lake and on the Kennyville Stage, near Noah's Ark. Ethnic days at Kennywood are a century-old tradition and are held throughout the year. The Fall Fantasy parade is held each August.

Bushkill Park

OPENED 1902

WHEN NEAL FEHNEL, A.K.A. BALLOONS THE CLOWN, WAS PRESENTED WITH the opportunity to purchase Bushkill Park in 1990, he didn't think he could come up with the money. For several months, Fehnel had been looking for a place to open a children's play center and banquet facility, and Bushkill Park had been searching for a buyer. But after some consideration, he found a partner, and he and William Hogan purchased the park. So began what could best be described as a true labor of love.

On the Shores of Bushkill Creek

While Bushkill Park has changed from its early days, it still retains the nostalgic atmosphere that likely attracted the Easton and Nazareth Rail Company at the turn of the twentieth century. The company, like others of the era, sought to build a resort at the end of its line to stimulate ridership on weekends and evenings. They found a 13-acre site about 3 miles north of Easton in Forks Township, situated on a U-shaped bend of Bushkill Creek. A millrace or stream connected the legs of the U, forming an island, on which the park was situated. A grain mill in what is now Bushkill Park's parking lot, powered by the millrace, was the park's neighbor until the 1940s.

Bushkill Park officially opened on July 3, 1902, after two years of planning. While the Easton and Nazareth Rail Company owned the property, the Hay Trolley Line, owned by Northampton Transit Company, operated the facility. The park's attractions consisted of a boat ride on Bushkill Creek,

Bushkill Park
2100 Bushkill Park Dr.
Easton, PA 18042
610-258-6941
www.bushkillpark.com

The pagoda was an early landmark and for a few years had a slide winding around the building. AUTHOR'S COLLECTION

a two-story building holding a dance hall and roller-skating rink, a primitive movie theater, pony rides, a small zoo, a swimming pool, picnic groves, and a refreshment stand built like a pagoda with five tiers. The top level of the pagoda had a circular slide that dropped to ground level. The park also featured a carousel with a primitive electrical system. To operate the carousel, a wire was placed in salt water, which generated electrical current. The farther the wire was put in the water, the faster the carousel went.

During these early days, Bushkill's most enduring attraction debuted when a two-story building was constructed in the heart of the park. Sometime before 1935, the building was converted into a fun house, and it remains in operation as the oldest functioning fun house in America.

The park added its largest ride in 1923, when a wooden roller coaster called the Comet was constructed. The ride traveled the entire length of the park, starting at the ballroom and running along the creek to the other side, where the carousel was located. Originally, it crossed the creek at this point before turning around to return to the station, but later it was modified to turn before the creek to cut down on maintenance costs. The opening of the Comet marked the high point of Bushkill Park. But tough times came in 1928, when the dance hall and roller rink

LOCATION

Bushkill Park is located about 3 miles from downtown Easton. From U.S. Route 22, exit onto PA Route 248, the Wilson–25th Street exit, and go north about a mile to Park Avenue. Turn right on Park Avenue (by Palmer Park Mall), go 1 mile, and turn right over the bridge. Bushkill Park will be on your right.

OPERATING SCHEDULE

Bushkill Park opens at noon on weekends from Memorial Day through mid-June, and Wednesday through Sunday from mid-June through Labor Day.

ADMISSION

Parking is free, and admission is free during the week. There is a nominal admission charge on weekends and holidays. Ride passes or individual ride tickets are available. Games, miniature golf, the roller rink, and Fascination Station cost extra. During some special events, admission is available only with a ride pass.

FOOD

Bushkill Park has two food stands: The Refreshment Stand offering hot dogs, hamburgers, french fries, pierogies, and pork roll; and the Fun Food Stand, near kiddieland, with ice cream, popcorn, candy apples, and cotton candy.

FOR CHILDREN

Bushkill Park's kiddieland, next to the main entrance, features nine rides, including a miniature roller coaster, a small merry-go-round, boats, and pony carts. Most of the other rides at Bushkill Park can be enjoyed by the entire family.

Fascination Station, targeted for kids up to age twelve, is open year-round and can be rented for parties.

SPECIAL FEATURES

Bushkill Park is a throwback to the way amusement parks used to be. The park features the last old-fashioned fun house in the United States, complete with a revolving barrel and a large wooden slide. The Pretzel is considered the oldest operating dark ride in the country.

The kiddieland is a veritable museum of antique kiddie rides, all of which have been lovingly restored. Several rides, including the Roto Whip and kiddie coaster, were manufactured by the W. F. Mangels Company, the earliest manufacturer of kiddie rides. The swan swing is also one of the earliest examples of a kiddie ride.

TIME REQUIRED

Bushkill Park can be enjoyed in about four hours, although small children might want to spend the entire day.

TOURING TIPS

Visit during the week, when admission is free.

burned down. By now, the trolley company was losing interest in the park and did not reconstruct the building.

The Depression hurt business further, and around 1933, the park was leased to Tom Long, who had more than twenty years' experience operating area amusement parks. Long came from a distinguished amusement park family that not only operated amusement parks, but also manufactured carousels. His brother Robert operated Eldridge Park in Elmira, New York; his brother Edward operated a carousel at Seneca Park in Rochester, New York; and his cousin George owned Sea Breeze Park, also in Rochester.

Under Long's leadership, Bushkill Park became a modern amusement park. He immediately rebuilt the skating rink/dance hall building, improved the swimming pool, replaced the original carousel with a dark ride from Pretzel Amusement Company, and added a carousel built in 1903 by the Long family. It had forty-six wooden animals and four chariots carved by Muller and Leopold. Music was provided by two band organs. The ride was originally installed at Burlington Island Park in New Jersey, and then moved to Island Park in Easton around 1912. It stayed there until the park closed in 1919 or 1920, and was then moved to Oakland Park in Bethlehem, Pennsylvania, before Tom Long brought it to Bushkill Park.

Long bought, restored, and resold carousels during the off-season throughout his career, and he occasionally substituted a choice animal for one on his carousel. As a result, the Bushkill Park carousel had sev-

The Comet roller coaster operated from 1923 to 1967. COLLECTION OF RON LONG

The Long carousel was originally assembled in 1903 and operated at Bushkill Park from 1933 until 1989. COLLECTION OF RON LONG

eral examples of the best work of Dentzel and Philadelphia Toboggan Company carvers. Long's restored carousels were sent to such faraway locations as Toronto, Canada, and Caracas, Venezuela.

With business improving, Long bought the property from the trolley company around 1939. Between 1935 and 1955, he added several rides: a whip from Mangels, bumper cars from Lusse, a Tilt-A-Whirl, a Flying Scooter, a train, and several kiddie rides, including airplanes, boats, swinging swans, a kiddie coaster, and pony carts, the last three of which are still in operation.

In the mid-1950s, the park added the Merry Mixer, which resembles the more common Scrambler and was built for Bushkill by the owner of nearby Indian Trail Park. Long exchanged a carousel for the ride. The park also built a kiddie merry-go-round, with aluminum horses and spinning tubs.

Around 1960, the Flying Scooter was converted into a new ride called Gemini 9, the airplane cars being replaced with cages in which the riders rode.

Bushkill Park has a great collection of vintage kiddie rides.

After Tom Long's death in 1965, the park was operated by his widow, Mabel, and Melvin Heavener, a longtime associate of Long's. Several kiddie rides joined the lineup around this time, including the Turtles, a miniwhip, and Sky Fighters. The aging Comet was removed after the 1967 season. At this point, Mabel Long briefly considered selling the park to the city of Easton to be converted into a municipal park, but the deal did not go anywhere, and in 1968, a Wild Mouse roller coaster was purchased from nearby Dorney Park to replace the Comet.

The 1970s were a quiet decade for Bushkill Park, although high maintenance and insurance costs, along with dwindling profits, forced the park to close its pool around 1978. In 1979, Bushkill Creek flooded and ruined the stunts in the dark ride. Lacking the funds to fully restore the ride, the park briefly renamed it the Ripp Off. No one complained!

By the 1980s, Bushkill found it increasingly difficult to compete against larger parks and their flashy rides, and was losing industrial picnics because of area factory closings. In 1985, the millrace was eliminated, ending Bushkill Park's days as an island. The following year, Heavener died, after fifty-five years at the park. Mabel Long continued to run the park until her death in 1989 at the age of eighty-two.

Now the park's future was very much in doubt. Long's heirs either were not interested in operating the park or lacked the resources to undertake the needed renovations, and as a result, Bushkill Park was placed on the market. Over the next several months, they searched for a buyer. Several potential deals fell through, and the park opened for one day on April 29, 1990, for a nursery school picnic.

A New Beginning

At that time, Neal Fehnel, a professional clown, was searching for a space to set up a banquet and entertainment facility. William Hogan, a business acquaintance, steered him to the shuttered amusement park, and the two teamed up to purchase the facility. But they lacked the resources to purchase Bushkill's crown jewel, the antique carousel.

The Long family searched for a buyer who would purchase the carousel, keep it intact, and place it back in operation in the Easton area. Despite their best efforts, and spirited fund-raising by some concerned citizens, local municipalities could not find a mutually agreeable place for the carousel to be operated or establish who would maintain it. After more than a year of trying to find a local home, they finally sold it in 1991 to an entrepreneur in Ohio who promised to keep the carousel intact and not sell off the animals separately, which was a major concern of the heirs.

The situation at Bushkill Park was more optimistic. On August 25, 1990, Fehnel and Hogan opened the park for a one-day open house. Because the rides needed maintenance, only the skating rink, picnic groves, and concessions were open.

After being closed for most of 1990, the new owners had their work cut out for them. The rides were run down, the electrical system was in need of replacement, and everything needed a coat of paint. But the park held special memories for generations of local residents who wanted to see Bushkill Park thrive again, and more than thirty volunteers stepped forward to prepare the park for the 1991 season. A local electrician upgraded the wiring, and various companies donated materials such as pipe, paint, and a forklift.

That first season was a learning experience for the new owners. "The park ran us," says Fehnel. But they were encouraged enough to continue improvements. In November 1991, Fascination Station opened in the former park arcade. This was the entertainment center Fehnel initially sought to open and features a ball pit, a moon bounce, and games.

The outlook for Bushkill Park was brighter than it had been in decades, but Fehnel and Hogan knew that the park would not be complete until a replacement was located for the carousel. In 1993, they located an antique carousel that had sat forlornly at Willow Mill Park near Harrisburg, Pennsylvania, since that park closed in 1989. Manufactured around 1915 by the Allan Herschell Company of North

Tonawanda, New York, the ride has forty-two wooden horses and two chariots. It came to Willow Mill during the Depression from Fort Wayne, Indiana. Bushkill Park's timing was perfect, as within hours after the carousel was moved out of Willow Mill Park, an adjacent river flooded and engulfed its former home.

Ron Long, a nephew of Tom and Mabel's, teamed up with Fehnel and Hogan to acquire the ride and coordinate restoration. Long now owns the carousel and leases it to Bushkill Park on an exclusive basis. It needed a lot of work after sitting exposed to the elements for four years. Pieces were missing, layers of paint obscured original details, and some horses had nails in them from past repair jobs. For fifteen months, forty-nine volunteers assisted Long in restoring the machine, and on Memorial Day 1994, the carousel opened to the music of an antique Wurlitzer band organ. The carousel has become a particular source of pride for Ron Long, who carries on his family's tradition of overhauling carousels by maintaining the mechanism and keeping the animals on Bushkill's carousel repaired and painted.

Bill Hogan sold his interest to Sam Baurkot in 1996. Fehnel opened a chocolate factory next to Fascination Station in 1997, reflecting his love for candy. Here visitors can enjoy homemade chocolates and other treats. In 2000, the park brought back the brass ring dispenser on the carousel in honor of Bushkill's ninety-eighth birthday.

The park has continued to improve, and with the dawn of a new century, Bushkill Park has truly returned to its former glory. New rides are still being added, including two new kiddie rides.

The Barl of Fun has been an attraction since Bushkill's earliest years.

The Haunted Pretzel is one of the oldest dark rides in the country.

Bushkill Park Today

Bushkill Park remains an exquisite example of what an amusement park used to be. Towering trees shade an old-fashioned midway surrounded by rides and concessions. The park features eighteen rides, including nine for kids, along with miniature golf, the Fascination Station play area, a fun house, and a roller rink.

Most of the park's attractions are clustered around the main midway, which runs from the roller rink to the Pretzel dark ride. Here visitors can find the kiddieland, fun house, carousel, train, food concessions, and games. Expansive picnic groves surround the midway. There is live entertainment on the midway and the stage throughout the year.

Hersheypark

OPENED 1907

AT HERSHEYPARK, THE AROMA OF CHOCOLATE FILLS THE AIR. VISITORS are greeted by giant living Hershey Bars, Reese's Peanut Butter Cups, and Hershey Kisses, and are assigned a Hershey's brand to signify which rides they are tall enough to go on. Of course, the gift shops are full of chocolate. This is Hersheypark, the largest amusement park in Pennsylvania. Like the candy company, which continues to dominate the town, it is a living legacy of one man: Milton S. Hershey.

A Different Kind of Company Town

Milton Hershey gained his first taste of the candy business in 1876, when he opened a candy shop in Philadelphia. Though he had only a fourth-grade education, and this first business venture was unsuccessful, he kept trying and eventually succeeded in 1886, when he opened a caramel manufacturing company in Lancaster, Pennsylvania. During a trip to the World's Columbian Exposition in Chicago in 1893, he became entranced with German chocolate-making machinery and soon began producing chocolate at his Lancaster factory. Seeing a bright future in chocolate, he sold his caramel factory for $1 million in 1900 and set out to build the world's greatest chocolate manufacturing plant.

Hersheypark
100 West Hersheypark Dr.
Hershey, PA 17033-2797
1-800-HERSHEY
www.hersheypa.com

In 1903, he built a factory near his boyhood home east of Harrisburg, where there was an abundance of dairy farms to supply his new plant. As was common at the time, Hershey surrounded the factory with a company town. Rather than one of the faceless company towns of the era, Hershey constructed a "real hometown," with tree-lined streets, neat brick homes, a community center, a bank, and a department store. Along Spring Creek, which ran through town, he built a modest recreation area, which officially opened in 1907 with a baseball game on the athletic field attended by Hershey and his wife. The park also featured boating in the creek, picnic grounds, a bandstand, and a dancing pavilion that had been constructed in 1904.

The future of the park was set the following season, when Hershey's business manager, at the urging of one of the company's salesmen, purchased a used carousel for $1,500. Manufactured by Herschell Spillman of North Tonawanda, New York, the ride first opened on the Fourth of July. At 5 cents a ride, it brought in $87 the first day and $556 by the end of the season. Hershey immediately became enamored with the ride, and for years he was often spotted riding it and the park's succeeding carousels after the park had closed for the day. He even permitted local children to join him, as long as they behaved.

Starting in 1909, Hershey began to promote the new resort by placing postcards of Hersheypark and the town of Hershey in Hershey Bars. Millions of these cards were distributed, and soon Hersheypark was almost as famous as the candy.

The popularity of the carousel prompted Hershey to seek other rides for the growing resort, and in 1910, an electric miniature railway was constructed to provide transportation throughout the shaded grounds. It

SCENE IN HERSHEY PARK – HERSHEY, PA.
Home of the Hershey Chocolate Co.

A placid Hersheypark was featured in this chocolate bar postcard in the early 1900s.
AUTHOR'S COLLECTION

SOME OF THE AMUSEMENTS IN HERSHEY PARK
Home of the Hershey Chocolate Co., Hershey, Pa.

The miniature train and carousel were Hersheypark's first two rides. AUTHOR'S
COLLECTION

became one of the park's most enduring and beloved attractions, carrying millions of passengers before being retired in 1972.

Although originally intended for company employees, Hersheypark's close proximity to trolley and railroad lines soon made the park a regional destination. The growing crowds prompted the park to add a new carousel in 1912. Built by Gustav Dentzel of Philadelphia, the ride was a huge improvement over the original carousel and featured fifty-two hand-carved animals. It was placed in a new building along Spring Creek. Growth continued with the construction of a large convention center, which now houses the Hershey Museum, in 1915, and the thousand-seat Hershey Café, a favorite hangout of Milton Hershey, in 1916.

The park stagnated for several years in the face of World War I and financial problems for Milton Hershey. But with a brightening financial picture and the approaching twentieth anniversary of the town in 1923, Hershey decided to add a flashy new attraction. Built by the Philadelphia Toboggan Company, the Joy Ride, soon known as the Wildcat, was a 2,000-foot-long wooden roller coaster that bridged Spring Creek and featured several large drops. The Wildcat caused such a sensation on opening day that the Hershey *Press* reported that riders "almost swamped ticket takers in order to have a ride. . . . So well did the trip appeal to them, that it was necessary to dislodge a number by use of a crowbar to give others a chance." As was the local custom at the time,

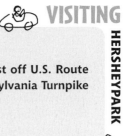

LOCATION

Hersheypark is located about 15 miles west of Harrisburg, just off U.S. Route 322. The park is easily accessible from Exit 266 of the Pennsylvania Turnpike (I-76) or Exit 80 (PA Route 743) of I-81.

OPERATING SCHEDULE

Hersheypark is open at 10 A.M. weekends in May and September and daily from Memorial Day weekend through Labor Day. Closing time varies by time of year. The park is also open weekends in late October for Hersheypark in the Dark, and on selected days from mid-November through New Year's for Christmas Candy-lane, which features about a dozen operating rides and thousands of lights adorning the grounds.

ADMISSION

Pay-one-price admission of under $40 entitles visitors to all rides and attractions, with the exception of the paddle boats, for which there is an additional nominal fee. Parking and games also cost extra.

   During the Christmas Candylane and other selected off-season events, admission is free and rides are priced individually.

FOOD

Hersheypark features over fifty different food concessions, ranging from Pippin's, a sit-down restaurant, to chain food outlets, to strolling vendors selling lemonade and popcorn. Minetown Vittles is the park's largest facility and offers indoor seating. Nearby is the Loft, a food court. Kosher food is available at Central PA's Kosher Mart in Rhineland.

FOR CHILDREN

Few parks in the world have more kiddie rides than Hersheypark, which features twenty-one kiddie rides, including Tiny Timbers, a scaled-down log flume; two kiddie trains; and classics such as a whip, named Wells Cargo, a merry-go-round, and the Lady Bug, a small-scale Tumble Bug. The kiddie rides are scattered throughout the grounds rather that being clustered in a single kiddieland. The largest concentrations are in the Music Box Way and Carrousel Circle areas, with smaller concentrations in Midway America, Minetown, and Pioneer Frontier.

SPECIAL FEATURES

Though Hersheypark does not have a chocolate theme, the presence of the sweet treat is never far from your mind, with the ever-present aroma, the abundance of chocolate in the gift shops, and the costumed characters representing favorite Hershey brands. Even the park's height limitation system is keyed to the Hershey products.

(continued on page 142)

No amusement park in Pennsylvania, and few in the country, has more rides than Hersheypark. These range from classic favorites, such as the carousel and the railroad, to modern thrillers such as the Tidal Force.

Hersheypark also has more roller coasters than any other park in Pennsylvania, including the Comet, a classic woodie; the Wildcat, a modern adaptation of a 1920s twister roller coaster; the Lightning Racer, a double-track ride; the Great Bear, in which riders travel beneath the track; sooperdooperlooper, the first looping roller coaster in the eastern United States; the Sidewinder, in which the train travels forward and backward; Roller Soaker, a wet adventure; and the Trailblazer and Wild Mouse for the family.

TIME REQUIRED

To fully enjoy Hersheypark, you'll need to spend at least one day. One-, two-, and three-day tickets are available.

TOURING TIPS

If you have kids, visit the Ride Operations Office to get them measured. They will receive a wristband showing their height category so they don't have to be measured at each ride.

Try to visit on a weekday before mid-June, as the park tends to be less crowded. Arrive early, and head straight to Midway America or Minetown in the back of the park.

Don't miss Chocolate World, right outside the front gate, offering a free ride through the chocolate-making process. The air-conditioned building also has a restaurant, food court, and huge gift shop selling a full array of Hershey products. Its chocolate milkshakes are legendary. Most people visit Chocolate World first thing in the morning, so try to visit during the middle of the day, when the park is the hottest and most crowded.

The town of Hershey is full of other activities that can fill a weekend, including Zoo America and the Hershey Museum. Zoo America admission is free with your Hersheypark admission, although there is a fee for the museum.

women were not allowed to board until the afternoon, so the first riders were all men.

The Wildcat kicked off a period of growth for Hersheypark. The park added its first two kiddie rides in 1926. In 1929, a Mill Chute ride, a forerunner of today's log flume rides, was constructed, and a new swimming pool replaced the one built in 1910. The bathhouse of the original pool was turned into a fun house in 1930.

Surviving Tough Times

Unlike most amusement parks, which were struggling to survive during the Depression, Hersheypark thrived. Business at the candy factory remained strong, as candy bars represented a cheap indulgence, and the free candy factory tours were a popular attraction for people seeking inexpensive diversions.

But most important, Milton Hershey, who by now had become a well-known philanthropist, launched the Great Building Campaign as a way to put local men to work. Starting in 1932, Hershey used his wealth to transform the town, reviving plans that had been put on hold during World War I. Many of the town's largest buildings were constructed, including the opulent Hotel Hershey and Hershey Community Center in 1933; the Hershey Industrial School in 1934; the Hersheypark Arena, built in 1936 after Milton Hershey was turned away from a sold-out hockey game in the Convention Center; Hershey Gardens in 1937; and Hershey Stadium in 1939.

With so many local people working, Hersheypark also thrived. An elaborate sunken garden, featuring a huge fountain, was constructed between the pool and ballroom in 1932, and in 1933, the Mill Chute was renovated with a taller, steeper drop. On July 4, 1934, Hersheypark hosted the largest crowd in its history, with sixty thousand visitors.

World War II was also a prosperous time for the town and its amusement park, as Hershey Bars were a staple in the rations being shipped overseas to the troops. But in 1943, wartime rationing meant that cars could not be driven to Hersheypark. As a result, the ballroom was closed, and the

The Mill Chute was a favorite until Hurricane Agnes destroyed it in 1972. AUTHOR'S COLLECTION

park did not open on Mondays. In 1944, with the situation improving, the ballroom reopened, although the park remained closed on Mondays.

That year, Hersheypark acquired its current carousel, a large, four-row model manufactured in 1919 by the Philadelphia Toboggan Company. The ride, originally built for Liberty Heights Park in Baltimore, features sixty-six horses, two chariots, and almost eighteen hundred lights, nearly five times the number on the park's previous one. The carousel had been carved immediately after World War I and was adorned with patriotic carvings. Hersheypark extensively rehabbed the ride before reopening, painting all the horses chocolate brown. It has since been restored to its original colors.

The carousel turned out to be the last ride Milton Hershey purchased, as he died on October 13, 1945. He had developed a special fondness for his amusement park and was often seen strolling the grounds picking up litter, with the exception of Hershey Bar wrappers, which he left on the ground face up.

Hershey's successors continued to upgrade the park. They launched the largest expansion in its history in 1946. Given that the aging Wildcat was in need of extensive renovation, it was decided to replace the ride with a larger, faster coaster. The result was the Comet, an 84-foot-tall,

Hersheypark is full of roller coasters, including the sooperdooperlooper (lower left), Great Bear (far left and center), and Comet (top).

2,950-foot-long ride that started out with an 80-foot plunge over Spring Creek, followed by a second, 70-foot drop toward the creek. The T-shaped ride changed the look of the park and remains a favorite to this day.

Following the opening of the Comet, Hersheypark entered a quiet time, with minimal expansion, although, as in most parks, all of the park's kiddie rides were moved into separate kiddieland in 1949. As the 1950s ended, Hersheypark was facing a changing world. With the opening of Disneyland in 1955, theme parks and their larger, more elaborate rides were spreading throughout the country. The park responded by adding similar rides, including the Dry Gulch Railroad and a large Turnpike ride along the creek in 1961. Starship America, which resembled Disney's famous Rocket Jets, was added in 1962. The park hired the great dark ride designer William Tracy to theme the Mill Chute as the Lost River in 1963 and convert the 1930s vintage Pretzel dark ride to the Golden Nugget dark ride in 1964. Other theme-park-style rides were added as well. The Skyview sky ride debuted in 1966 and the Monorail in 1969. The Monorail was built as a joint venture between Hersheypark and Hershey Chocolate to help relieve the increasingly heavy traffic traveling through town to the candy factory. The 5,380-foot-long ride made stops at the amusement park and in town near the factory.

By now Hersheypark was a successful midsize amusement park. But with theme parks opening at an increasing rate, many parks like Hersheypark were closing, and even Hersheypark was having problems. The pool closed in 1967 in the face of skyrocketing maintenance bills, the ballroom was used only sporadically because of changing musical tastes, many rides were aging, buildings needed maintenance, and the open admission policy was starting to cause security problems.

Hersheypark was at a crossroads. Management had to decide whether to improve the park or close it and redevelop the land for more passive uses. They chose to keep the park open and, in 1969, hired Randall Duell, the most successful theme park designer of the era, to develop a master plan to revamp Hersheypark.

A New Hersheypark

Changes began slowly. The park was fenced in and admission charged for the first time in 1971. In 1972, the renovation kicked into high gear. Plans were announced for a five-year redevelopment that would organize the park into a series of themed areas, construct new buildings, and add the larger rides that were considered the standard in the theme park era.

The 1972 season saw the development of Carrousel Circle on the former ballfield next to the Comet. The centerpiece of the area is the park's carousel, which was relocated from the shore of Spring Creek into a festive new building. Joining the carousel were six new smaller rides. Linking Carrousel Circle to the existing park was Der Deitch Platz, another theme area offering Pennsylvania Dutch crafts.

In June 1972, Hurricane Agnes inundated the park. Spring Creek overflowed its banks, washing away cars from the Turnpike ride, destroying the Animal Garden petting zoo, and so severely damaging the Lost River mill chute that it never reopened. The dolphins, which had taken up residence in the new Aqua Theater, had to be relocated to a local swimming pool.

But Hersheypark barely missed a beat, and the redevelopment kicked into high gear for the 1973 season. Replacing the pool and sunken gardens were two new themed areas, Tudor Square and Rhineland, which formed a new entrance to the park next to Carrousel Circle. Hersheypark also added two major rides. In Carrousel Circle, a 130-foot-tall double Ferris wheel provided a panoramic view of the redeveloping park, and the former site of the bandstand, which was built in 1914, became home to the Coal Cracker, a large flume ride. Nearby, a new amphitheater for live shows was built on the same site as Hersheypark's original amphitheater, which operated from 1908 to 1965.

For years, ever larger crowds choked the factory and the town of Hershey, and in the increasingly competitive chocolate market, trade secrets could not be revealed to the general public. As a result, factory tours were discontinued in 1972 and replaced by Chocolate World. Located at the entrance to Hersheypark, Chocolate World features food service areas, gift shops, and a ride through a simulated chocolate factory.

By now, Hersheypark was a different park than it had been just a few years earlier. While great care was taken to preserve as many of the stately old trees as possible, the redevelopment meant the end of many longtime traditions, such as the pool, ballroom, sunken garden, Golden Nugget dark ride, miniature railway, and picnic pavilions. But patrons responded well to the improvements, and attendance in 1973 broke one million for the first time.

The energy crisis forced Hersheypark to scale back expansion in 1974, although two major rides did debut: a 1,268-foot-long Skyride linking Rhineland with the back of the park, until the ride was removed in 1992, and the Trailblazer roller coaster, a 1,874-foot-long, 43-foot-tall family roller coaster built into a ravine.

Expansion in 1975 concentrated on a 4-acre parcel in the back of the park. In addition to two new Turnpike rides that replaced the original one, the new area was anchored by the Kissing Tower, a 330-foot-tall observation tower with windows in the shape of Hershey's Kisses. The hilltop location was a natural for this towering attraction, as it is the highest point in the park. The growing height of the tower during construction created problems in town, as onlookers slowed to view the construction, causing traffic accidents. As a result, the park posted caution signs around the park reading, "Caution, traffic is slowing 'cause the tower is growing."

In 1977, the park unveiled a spectacular new roller coaster, sooperdooperlooper. Built adjacent to the Comet, the $2 million ride is 2,615 feet long, stands 85 feet tall, and was the first roller coaster in the eastern United States to feature a loop. The ride created such a sensation that Hersheypark was forced to close its gates for the first time in history on July 23, after twenty-five thousand people packed the park. By the end of the season, total attendance hit 1.7 million—more than twice the attendance just ten years before.

Hersheypark's parent company, HERCO, spent much of the 1980s expanding its operations outside Hershey, developing hotels, and even taking over operation of Lake Compounce, an amusement park in Bristol, Connecticut, in 1985.

With company funds being diverted elsewhere, expansion at Hersheypark slowed, and much of the attention was placed on developing the new Pioneer Frontier themed area. This new area became home to most of Hersheypark's new water attractions, including Canyon River Rapids, a $4 million, 1,700-foot-long river rapids attraction in 1987, and the Frontier Chute Out, a $1 million complex of four water slides in 1988. In 1991, Sidewinder opened in Pioneer Frontier—the park's first new roller coaster in fourteen years.

A New Era of Growth

By now, HERCO was retrenching and divesting its assets outside of town, and all the company's resources were focused on Hersheypark, leading to a period of significant growth. This new era kicked off in 1994, with the addition of Tidal Force, a 100-foot-tall, $4 million splash-water ride. In 1996, Hersheypark honored its traditional roots by adding a new 8-acre themed area called Midway America, a tribute to amusement parks of yesteryear. The first phase, opening in 1996, consisted of the Wildcat, a $5.5 million, 90-foot-tall wooden roller coaster built in the style of the classic 1920s twister roller coasters with twelve steeply banked turns and twenty track crossovers along its 3,200 feet. The Wildcat was the first major project of Great Coasters International of Sunbury, Pennsylvania. It was a huge success, and that year, park attendance exceeded 2 million for the first time.

The next phase of Midway America opened for Hersheypark's ninetieth anniversary in 1997. Three kiddie rides were relocated from else-

The Wildcat is modeled after the twisting rides of the 1920s.

where in the park, and two major new rides were constructed: a 100-foot-tall Ferris wheel and the first whip ride manufactured in several decades. Built by Ride Works of Sarasota, Florida, the new whip is nearly identical to the classic manufactured by the William Mangels Company of Brooklyn, from 1918 until the 1950s.

Expansion moved to the other end of the park in 1998, with the addition of the Great Bear, a $13 million roller coaster from the noted Swiss firm of Bolliger & Mabillard. The ride represents a new generation of roller coasters in which riders are suspended underneath the tracks. This added an extra thrill, given the Great Bear's location winding along and above Spring Creek and through existing attractions, including sooperdooperlooper and Coal Cracker. The 2,800-foot-long Great Bear features a 124-foot first drop, four inversions, and a top speed of 58 miles per hour.

The following season, the summer-long Hersheypark Fair was born. A 10,000-square-foot festival tent housed a revolving series of special events, and five new rides were added, including a Wild Mouse roller coaster.

After adding three roller coasters in the past four seasons, Hersheypark had established itself as a roller coaster capital, and it did not intend to let that reputation slip in 2000. The result was the addition of the 90-foot-tall Lightning Racer, an immense $12.5 million wooden roller coaster that features two separate tracks named Thunder and Lightning. Riders race each other along 3,400 feet of track at speeds up to 51 miles per hour, seeming to narrowly escape collision several times.

Your favorite Hershey treats come to life at Hersheypark. PHOTO BY HERSHEYPARK

By now, Hersheypark had a well-established reputation in the industry for its ability to adapt and thrive in a changing industry, and in late 2000, the park received the Applause Award, the industry's highest honor.

Hersheypark's newest attraction combines the two most popular rides found at any amusement park: roller coasters and water rides. Opening in 2002, Roller Soaker consists of a 1,300-foot-long, 70-foot-high roller coaster. Riders travel suspended under the track and are sprayed with water cannons by park visitors and Hershey characters—but riders have their own water cannons to retaliate.

Hersheypark Today

Hersheypark today is the largest amusement park in Pennsylvania. On its rolling, tree-shaded grounds are sixty rides, including twenty-one for kids, in eight different themed areas.

Tudor Square is Hersheypark's main entrance area and is home to Pippin's restaurant, a gourmet coffee shop, and the Chocolate House gift shop. Rhineland is just past the front gate and features a variety of shops and concessions. Just beyond Rhineland is Carrousel Circle. The park's magnificent antique carousel is the centerpiece of this area and is surrounded by family rides such as the Giant Wheel and Scrambler, as well as a wide array of kiddie rides.

Comet Hollow is located along the shores of Spring Creek and is dominated by the Comet and sooperdooperlooper roller coasters, along with games and concessions. Minetown is on top of a hill overlooking Comet Hollow. This area holds two of the park's largest food service facilities—Minetown Restaurant and the Loft—along with the Great Bear roller

The Lightning Racer is actually two separate rides.

The author's son demonstrates Hershey-park's unique height measurement system. He's a Reese's Peanut Butter Cup.

coaster, Coal Cracker flume, and Kissing Tower, which provides a spectacular view of the park and surrounding countryside. Live entertainment takes place in the amphitheater, and the Aqua Theater hosts Hersheypark's dolphin show.

Music Box Way is also next to Comet Hollow and features seven kiddie rides, Dry Gulch Railroad, the monorail, and the Music Box Theater. Music Box Way leads into Pioneer Frontier, where most of Hersheypark's water rides are located, including Canyon River Rapids, Tidal Force, and Roller Soaker. Changing facilities are available for those who don't want to get their street clothes soaked. The Trailblazer and Sidewinder roller coasters are also found in Pioneer Frontier.

Midway America is Hersheypark's newest themed area. A tribute to the golden age of amusement parks, Midway America features three roller coasters—the Lightning Racer, Wildcat, and Wild Mouse—along with such classics as a Ferris wheel, whip, Music Express, and the Merry Derry Dip Fun Slide.

DelGrosso's Amusement Park

OPENED 1909

THE SPIRIT OF DELGROSSO'S AMUSEMENT PARK IS SUMMARIZED IN THE sign at the front entrance: "The DelGrosso family welcomes you." Del-Grosso's is still run by the family that purchased it in 1946. The care they put into the operation is evident throughout the park, from the impeccably maintained rides to the nicest baby changing facility found in any amusement park. But above all, it is most evident in the food that they serve. Everything from spaghetti sauce to pizza dough is made from scratch in their cavernous kitchen. Overseeing the activity, for more than fifty years, is family matriarch Murf DelGrosso, whose potato salad has become so famous that on some days over 500 pounds are sold.

A Quiet Beginning

Since this is farm country, it is not surprising that the land on which Del-Grosso's Amusement Park is located was originally a farm. Starting in 1907, the owner Fred Bland would let a local carnival, owned by the Rinard Brothers, set up their rides on his farm during the summer. Seeing the crowds that the carnival attracted, Bland opened a small amusement park at the farm in 1909, building a dance hall and a picnic grove. The Rinards continued to provide rides.

DelGrosso's Amusement Park
Old Route 220
Tipton, PA 16684-0335
814-684-3538
www.delgrossos.com

Bland's Park, as it was then known, entered its first golden age in 1923, when the Tipton Speedway opened nearby. The speedway attracted people from throughout the region, who wanted to combine a day at the races with a visit to the amusement park.

With the increasing crowds, Bland sought to add some more permanent amusements and in 1924 purchased a new carousel from the Herschell Spillman Company of North Tonawanda, New York. The ride was carved by hand, with thirty-six horses and two chariots. It remains the park's most enduring feature.

The park was more successful than ever, and George Rinard, of the carnival family, purchased it from Fred Bland in 1928. But soon the Depression caused the speedway to close, and Bland's Park went into a long period of decline.

In the fall of 1946, Fred DelGrosso, a restaurateur from nearby Altoona, came across the run-down amusement park and purchased it on a whim. At the time, the park featured only a roller-skating rink, dance hall, bowling alley, picnic area, and five rides, including the carousel, a steam train, a Flying Scooter, and bumper cars.

Fred's wife, Mafalda, or Murf, recalls, "He didn't tell me for several months, and when he told me, I thought, what's he gonna do with this place?" She didn't even visit the park for two years. But upon moving there, she too became enamored with the little amusement park, and now dozens of DelGrosso family members work there.

The DelGrossos immediately went to work to upgrade the facility, adding rides, constructing new buildings, and introducing the park's live pony ride. The park became famous for its barbecued chicken dinners, still a picnic staple. Through the late 1950s and early 1960s, the park

DelGrosso's was a quiet roadside attraction in the early years. The carousel can be seen in the trees on the left. COLLECTION OF DELGROSSO'S AMUSEMENT PARK

The first train ride at DelGrosso's was steam-powered. COLLECTION OF DELGROSSO'S AMUSEMENT PARK

continued to grow, with the Ferris wheel and a kiddie roller coaster joining the park in 1957, a new steam train in 1960, and a kiddie Turnpike ride in 1962.

A Growing Enterprise

Although Bland's Park remained a popular getaway, further changes did not come until the 1980s. Two new rides were added in 1980, and two years later, the DelGrossos built a factory across the street from the park to manufacture their increasingly popular spaghetti sauce, which had been made in the park's kitchen since the late 1940s. This freed up space for additional expansion. In 1983, the Space Odyssey and two additional rides made their debut. For the Space Odyssey, a Caterpillar ride that the park had purchased in 1970 from nearby Lakemont Park was enclosed in a building, and an elaborate light and sound show was added. It remains one of the most popular rides in the park.

By now, business at Bland's Park was increasing significantly. The improvements were starting to pay off, and its main competitor, Lakemont Park, was having problems. It had undergone an unpopular transformation into the Boyertown theme park, and area residents were

LOCATION

DelGrosso's Amusement Park is located on Old Route 220 in Tipton, about 10 miles north of Altoona. The park is accessible from the Bellwood and Tipton-Grazierville exits of I-99 (Exits 41 and 45).

OPERATING SCHEDULE

DelGrosso's Amusement Park is open weekends in May and September, and daily from Memorial Day weekend through Labor Day. The water park and go-carts are the only attractions in operation on Mondays. On most days, the water park opens at 10 A.M., with the remaining attractions opening at noon.

ADMISSION

Parking and admission are free, with tickets sold for individual rides. All-day passes are also available for under $15 that permit access to the amusement park, water park, or both. Go-carts and live ponies are not included in any all-day pass and cost extra.

FOOD

DelGrosso's has ten food locations. Murf's Kitchen is the park's main food stand, serving sandwiches, hot dogs, burgers, steak sandwiches, hoagies, and the park's famous potato salad. Nearby is the Pizza Stand, with fresh-made pizzas. Tipton Creek is home to the Char Grill, featuring hot dogs, burgers, and chicken. There are also several food facilities on the east side of Route 220, including the Clubhouse and Austin's Texas Hot Dogs. You may also bring your own food into the park.

FOR CHILDREN

Kids Kingdom, located near the front of the amusement park, is the park's kiddieland, with eleven rides. The park also has many family rides, such as the carousel, train, and Ferris wheel, and a number of inexpensive, easy-to-win games, in which everyone wins a prize.

SPECIAL FEATURES

DelGrosso's Amusement Park is particularly proud of its antique carousel. Purchased new by the park in 1924, the carousel was manufactured by the Herschell Spillman Company and features thirty-six hand-carved horses. An antique Wurlitzer band organ provides the perfect musical accompaniment for the ride.

Few parks can match DelGrosso's for its high-quality, reasonably priced food. Everything is made from scratch at the park. Go hungry, and don't miss the pizza and potato salad.

(continued on page 156)

VISITING (continued from page 155)

TIME REQUIRED

The amusement park can be enjoyed in as little as four hours, but to experience all of the park's attractions, allow a full day.

TOURING TIPS

The water park opens two hours before the rest of the amusements, so start your day there, and move into the amusement park.

Discounted passes are available in the evening.

looking for an alternative. As a result, Bland's Park kicked off a five-year, $2.5 million improvement program that totally revamped the facility. New brick buildings replaced the old wooden ones, the gravel walkways were replaced with cement, unsightly overhead utility lines were buried, and in 1985, a series of free country concerts was started.

With the park's infrastructure rebuilt, attention was now turned to expanding the ride lineup. In 1987, Bland's replaced its aging bumper car ride with its first major roller coaster, the Zyklon, purchased from a defunct South Dakota amusement park. The steel track ride is 1,710 feet long and anchored the new, western-flavored Tipton Creek area, which

The carousel has been the park's most enduring attraction, operating since 1924.

The Zyklon was added in 1987.

was completed the following season with the addition of a miniature train and two other rides.

With several solid years of growth behind it, Bland's Park was now becoming increasingly constrained in its property on the west side of U.S. Route 220. As a result, the park built a new pedestrian bridge over the highway in 1989, connecting the amusement park on the west side of the highway with the east side, where the parking lot had been relocated two years earlier.

Bland's Park entered a new golden age in the 1990s. The decade kicked off with the addition of a new bumper car ride and two kiddie rides, and much of the decade was spent developing new attractions on the east side of the highway. The first attraction was an elaborate new miniature golf course in 1992, followed by two go-cart tracks in 1994. Responding to the increasing popularity of water parks, one of the go-cart tracks was replaced in 1997 by Tipton Waterworks, an elaborate water play area featuring a huge bucket that periodically dumped hundreds of gallons on spectators. Tipton Rapids, completed in 1999, consisted of five water slides extending from two towers 50 and 67 feet tall.

The original amusement park across the street was not forgotten, and a number of rides were added there during the decade as well, including the Casino in 1992, the Flying Bobs in 1994, a Round Up in 1995, and a new bumper car ride in 1996 to replace one crushed by heavy winter snows in 1994.

The midway at DelGrosso's. The entrance to Kids Kingdom can be seen in the background.

By the start of the twenty-first century, Bland's Park had established itself as a major amusement park in central Pennsylvania. The Del-Grossos decided that a new century called for a new image and changed the name of the park to DelGrosso's Amusement Park. The Flying Scooter was retired, and two new rides—the Sea Dragon and Balloon Race—made their debuts.

DelGrosso's Amusement Park Today

DelGrosso's Amusement Park has twenty-seven rides, including twelve for kids, along with a water park and a miniature golf course. The park is bisected by Old Route 220. On the east side of the road are the main parking lot; the main ticket booth; Tipton Waterworks and Tipton Rapids, featuring five water slides and a water play area; the Speedway go-cart track; and the Championship miniature golf course.

Across the bridge is the main amusement park. Located here are Kids Kingdom, with eleven kiddie rides, and the main midway, featuring the Carousel, Sea Dragon, Space Odyssey, Murf's Kitchen, the park gift shop, and most of the games. At the far end of the park is Tipton Creek, where you can find the Zyklon roller coaster, train ride, bumper cars, and pony rides.

Knoebels
Amusement Resort

OPENED 1926

IT'S A BEAUTIFUL SUMMER DAY IN NORTH-CENTRAL PENNSYLVANIA, AND a steady stream of traffic moves through the small town of Elysburg. The traffic seems out of place in this quiet part of the state, but it's just another day at Knoebels Amusement Resort, located in the hills just outside town. Cars by the hundreds head into the woods to the expansive parking lot, past the rides, concessions, and sprawling picnic groves. The park's free admission and parking, delicious food, and small-town atmosphere have made Knoebels a regional destination, and people travel from far and wide to enjoy its charms.

A Place to Cool Off

This land, located at the confluence of Mugser Run and Roaring Creek, had been a popular destination for years before Knoebels officially opened for business in 1926. In the early part of the twentieth century, Sunday afternoon hayrides visited the farm of Henry Hartman Knoebel, where the visitors enjoyed the cool waters of the creek. Knoebel dammed the creek with a "spring dam," so called because it had to be rebuilt every spring, to make it deep enough for swimming and for the daredevils who jumped off a covered bridge into the stream. While visitors enjoyed the creek, Knoebel would feed and water the horses for 25 cents.

Cottages for longer stays started appearing at the farm in 1917, and as the swimming hole

**Knoebels
Amusement Resort**
P.O. Box 317
Elysburg, PA 17824
570-672-2572
or 800-ITS-4FUN
www.knoebels.com

Knoebels swimming pool is where it all started in 1926. COLLECTION OF KNOEBELS AMUSEMENT RESORT

increased in popularity, Knoebel constructed picnic tables and benches and placed them throughout the grounds.

Business continued to increase, and in 1925, construction was started on a modern cement swimming pool with filtered water. The pool was ready by the following Fourth of July, when Knoebels Groves opened for business. An opening day advertisement described the pool as: "one of the largest and most sanitary pools in Central Pennsylvania. Supplied with real, honest to goodness pure water." Then as now parking and admission were free.

While the pool was the main attraction, the new park also featured a restaurant, some games, and its first ride, a used steam-powered carousel built by E. Joy Morris, an early manufacturer of carousels and roller coasters from Philadelphia.

The park grew slowly over the next several years. A small steam train ride through the woods was added, still in operation as the Old Smoky train, and a roller-skating rink, now the Roaring Creek Saloon, was built along the creek in 1934.

By the early 1940s, the park had outgrown the aging Morris carousel. In November 1941, Henry Knoebel located a magnificent carousel being sold by Riverside Park in Rahway, New Jersey, and purchased it for $4,000. Built in 1913 by George Kremers of Long Island, New York, the

 VISITING

KNOEBELS AMUSEMENT RESORT

LOCATION

Knoebels Amusement Resort lies between Elysburg and Catawissa on PA Route 487. From the east, take Exit 232 of I-80 onto Route 42 South to Route 487 South. From the west, take Exit 224 of I-80 onto PA Route 54 East through Danville. Cross the Susquehanna River bridge, turn left, and continue to follow Route 54 to Elysburg. Take PA Route 487 North to Knoebels.

OPERATING SCHEDULE

Knoebels Amusement Resort is open weekends in late April, May, and September and daily from the week before Memorial Day through Labor Day. Opening time is anywhere from 10 A.M. to noon, depending on the time of year. Closing time also varies.

ADMISSION

Admission and parking are free, with attractions priced on a pay-as-you-go basis, although Knoebels does offer a pay-one-price pass on weekdays and selected weekends. There are two kinds of passes, both less than $25, one of which excludes the two wooden roller coasters. The Haunted Mansion, miniature golf, Boat Tag, games, and pool cost extra.

FOOD

Knoebels is known for its reasonably priced, delicious home-cooked food. The park has nearly three dozen food facilities, ranging from sit-down restaurants to walk-up stands. The main restaurant, the Alamo, is famous for its chicken and waffles dinner. Next door is the Oasis Cafeteria, with daily specials. Other concessions include the Phoenix Junction steakhouse; the Roaring Creek Saloon, with southwestern food; Cesari's Pizza; the Old Mill ice cream parlor; and the International Food Court, with Mexican, Italian, and American specialties, including breakfast. You also may bring your own food into the park.

FOR CHILDREN

Most of the kiddie rides at Knoebels are clustered in one corner of the park. Among the fifteen kiddie rides are the Panther Cars, Fire Trucks, a whip, scaled-down bumper cars, handcars, and the sky slide.

The park also has a variety of family rides, including the Giant Wheel, two miniature trains, the Balloon Race, the High Speed Thrill Coaster, Motor Boats, and two antique carousels.

SPECIAL FEATURES

Knoebels takes pride in the fact that it has restored castoffs from other amusement parks to like-new condition. Throughout the park are rides, games, and other equipment from more than fifty different amusement parks. As a result,

(continued on page 162)

VISITING (continued from page 161)

Knoebels features several rides that are rare in today's parks, including the Motor Boats, Flyer, Satellite, Whipper, and Roto Jets.

The park is also known for its wooden roller coasters. The Phoenix gained national attention when it was relocated from Texas and rebuilt at Knoebels in 1985, and remains a favorite of enthusiasts for its abundance of "airtime." The Twister, one of the few roller coasters built by an amusement park rather than an outside firm, features large drops and high-speed turns.

Knoebels has a special affection for carousels. This is one of the few amusement parks in the world with two antique, hand-carved carousels, one of which, the Grand Carousel, allows riders to catch the brass rings, another amusement park tradition that has all but disappeared. Each carousel features two antique band organs, dating from the late 1800s and early 1900s, to provide music. Once common throughout the country, these intricate machines have become increasingly rare. In addition, Knoebels features a carousel museum and gift shop.

The Skooters is considered among enthusiasts to be the best bumper car ride found in any amusement park. The park continues to search out vintage Skooter cars manufactured by Lusse to provide a ride like the original.

TIME REQUIRED

Knoebels Amusement Resort is easily a full day's outing. If your time is limited, however, the park's free admission allows you to sample as many attractions as time permits.

huge, four-row ride features sixty-three horses and three chariots carved by Charles Carmel of Brooklyn.

Ten days after Knoebels acquired the carousel, Pearl Harbor was attacked, and America was drawn into World War II. Installation of the new carousel was delayed while the park struggled through the 1942 season and, because of gasoline rationing, failed to open for the 1943 season.

With the international situation brightening in 1944, Knoebels reopened, with its new carousel in place. By now the ride lineup was slowly expanding, with a small whip and a homemade kiddie airplane circular ride, in which each airplane was driven by small propellers.

The Park Grows

The end of World War II marked a new period of growth for Knoebels, and many of the features still enjoyed by today's visitors began to appear. The Playland arcade was constructed between the carousel and skating rink in 1946, followed by the park's now-famous Skooter ride in 1947. In

1944, the original restaurant was replaced by the Alamo. Still the park's main restaurant, the Alamo has become known for its home cooking and chicken and waffles dinner.

In the 1950s, Knoebels purchased several items from Croops Glen, a nearby amusement park that had gone out of business. One was a larger whip ride, called the Whipper, that replaced the original whip ride and is still in operation today. In 1955, Knoebels installed its first roller coaster, the High Speed Thrill Coaster, which stands 18 feet tall and has a 12-foot drop. Built by Overland Amusements of Saugus, Massachuetts, the steel-track roller coaster is powered by a six-cylinder Ford engine that propels the train uphill. The operator can adjust the speed of the chain to control the speed of the ride.

In the late 1950s, America was fascinated with the space race. In 1957, Knoebels responded with a primitive simulator attraction, more than twenty years before these were available elsewhere in the industry. The ride consisted of a large, homemade rocket lying on its side, modeled after an Atlas missile. Inside were several rows of bus seats and a rear-projection screen on which a 16-millimeter movie was shown, simulating a trip into outer space as the rocket tilted up and down. Knoebels shot aerial photos of the park and combined them with special effects put together by the team that created the special effects for the "Captain Video" television show. Each rider was given a "space meal" for their journey, a couple of Necco wafers said to be a hamburger, fries, and

The Stratoship was one of the park's early rides, operating from 1946 to 1955.
COLLECTION OF KNOEBELS AMUSEMENT RESORT

The rocket ship ride opened in 1957. In 1964, the park converted it into a slide.
COLLECTION OF KNOEBELS AMUSEMENT RESORT

milkshake condensed into pill form. Since man had not yet ventured into outer space, the ride was a huge success. But soon the novelty wore off, and in 1964, Knoebels tilted the rocket up on end and converted it into a large, circular slide that remains a park fixture.

The 1960s were a quiet decade for Knoebels. While some expansions took place, such as the opening of the campground in 1964 and the addition of the Roto Jet ride in 1965, the park focused on maintaining the existing attractions. Things started to pick up with the addition of the Paratrooper in 1970 and the Flyer in 1971, but soon the park faced a severe threat.

Coming Back Strong

Just as the 1972 season was reaching its peak, Hurricane Agnes hit Elysburg, and Roaring Creek spilled over its banks. By the next morning, most of the park was underwater.

When the waters receded, Knoebels was a mess. All but one of the park's twenty-five rides had been submerged; eighteen cottages were damaged beyond repair; the pool and motorboat pond were filled with mud; ride parts, picnic tables, trash cans, and benches were strewn throughout the park; all of the animals in the zoo were killed; and the arcade building was moved 6 feet from its original location, where it remains today.

Rather than close for the rest of the season, Knoebels was determined to reopen as soon as possible. Employees worked around the clock, and the park reopened ten days after the flood, although fourteen rides remained closed for repairs.

To demonstrate to the world that it had truly recovered from the flood, in 1973 the park built a major new signature attraction—a large Haunted Mansion dark ride. Built in a remote corner of the park, the ride was designed and constructed by the park staff, using parts obtained from amusement parks that were going out of business. The result was a highly popular ride that is continually being improved by the park and today is ranked as one of the top dark rides in the country.

In 1975, Knoebels paid tribute to its heritage by constructing a covered bridge in the heart of the park. Built using timbers from a 110-year-old gristmill, it commemorated the covered bridge that had served as a diving platform in the early years but was torn down in 1940.

As the park was nearing its golden anniversary in 1976, Knoebels came across a lost family heirloom, an antique carousel acquired by Lawrence Knoebel, Henry's son, in 1948. Smaller than the Grand Carousel, the two-row ride was built around 1910 by the noted firm of Stein & Goldstein and features twenty-eight hand-carved horses. The ride never operated at the park, but was taken to local carnivals by Lawrence before being sold to another amusement park in 1950. Knoebels restored the ride and placed it in the park's kiddieland for their fiftieth anniversary season.

The Haunted Mansion has become a favorite of enthusiasts around the world since its 1973 opening.

By now, about the only ride missing from Knoebels was a major roller coaster. Steel roller coasters were all the rage during the time, and the park located one for sale at Coney Island, New York. Built by well-known German roller coaster designer Anton Schwartzkopf, the Jet Star was 1,750 feet long and 44 feet high, featured a 40-foot drop, and reached a top speed of 35 miles per hour. According to Dick Knoebel, the Jet Star took the park to a new level, and attendance increased 20 percent during its first season in 1977.

Throughout its existence, Knoebels was a self-reliant park, depending on park staff to design and build new attractions. This creativity again came into play in 1978, when the park constructed the Cosmotron. The ride consisted of a Caterpillar, a ride in which a series of cars traveled along an undulating track surrounded by an elaborate light and sound show. The park purchased the Caterpillar from West View Park in Pittsburgh, which had closed the previous year. During the trip to Pittsburgh, when park staff saw West View's wooden roller coasters, they thought about moving one of them to Knoebels. But given the age and terrain-specific layout of West View's coasters, the idea was dropped, and the rides were demolished in 1981.

Achieving Recognition

Attention was now turned to other projects. Water slides were added to the pool in 1978 and 1979, and the bumper boat ride was built in 1982. By 1983, Knoebels had grown to the point where its patronage could support a large roller coaster. Although others in the industry encouraged them to add a steel-track looping roller coaster, the Knoebels staff still liked the idea of relocating a wooden roller coaster, and they began to look at the option more seriously. The Rocket, a ride built by the Philadelphia Toboggan Company in 1947, had been sitting abandoned at Playland in San Antonio, Texas, since the park closed in 1980. Knoebels finalized a deal to purchase the Rocket and, in early 1985, began dismantling the ride and transporting it to the park in Pennsylvania. Guided by Charles Dinn, an experienced roller coaster builder, reerection progressed rapidly. While two-thirds of the wood had to be replaced, primarily for new track, most of the vertical supports and mechanical hardware were retained. The project was completed for $1 million, half of what it would have cost to build a comparable-size wooden roller coaster from the ground up.

On June 5, the ride, renamed the Phoenix, after the mythical bird that rose from the ashes, opened to the public. The 3,100-foot-long, 78-foot-high ride changed the skyline of Knoebels and gained national recognition for the park.

The Phoenix took Knoebels to a whole new level when it opened in 1985.

Over the years, Knoebels had established a reputation in the industry for purchasing older rides from amusement parks that were closing or scaling back, and restoring them into like-new condition. As a result, the park had a unique atmosphere. The construction of the Phoenix was the pinnacle. By now, attendance was approaching a million people annually. Though the park still added used rides, such as a Galleon swinging ship in 1988 and an antique car ride that winds through the structure of the Phoenix in 1989, the limited capacity of most older rides meant that Knoebels had to start adding some higher-capacity contemporary rides.

Knoebels added the first such ride in 1990, constructing the Flume in an undeveloped area of the park beyond the Phoenix. Built by O. D. Hopkins, the leading log flume manufacturer of the era, it is a major ride occupying almost an acre and featuring 1,350 feet of water-filled trough, two major drops, and twelve turns.

Two years later, the park added a carousel museum. A one-of-a-kind attraction for an amusement park, the 4,000-square-foot museum features dozens of carousel horses from the Knoebel family collection, arranged in chronological order to show evolution of carousel carving. In the center of the room are several menagerie animals, and the walls are filled with carousel-related memorabilia. A special feature is one of the horses that operated on the park's original carousel, only one of two horses to survive a hurricane after the ride was sold in the early 1950s to a resort in the Poconos.

In 1993, an article praising the park's charms appeared in the Philadelphia *Inquirer*. Wire services picked it up, and soon people from coast to coast who had never heard of this mountain retreat knew about its unique atmosphere, free admission, and good food. People flocked to the park, which that year replaced the Jet Star with its first looping roller coaster, the 64-foot-tall Whirlwind, which flipped riders upside down twice.

Two new high-capacity rides debuted in 1994—a giant Ferris wheel, at 110 feet tall the tallest Ferris wheel in Pennsylvania, and the Italian Trapeze, a colorful swing ride.

Roaring Creek once again imperiled Knoebels in January 1996, when it flooded most of the park. Though parts of the park were washed away, damage was not as severe as in 1972, with much of it concentrated in the kiddie area. Again, Knoebels quickly repaired the damage.

By now, Knoebels had become the largest free-admission amusement park in America, and expansion accelerated. AXS, a modern spinning ride, opened in 1996, followed by Sklooosh, a 50-foot-tall splash-water ride in 1997. The name was said to be "the sound you hear from wet sneakers." Also added that year was the International Food Court, serving foods from around the world.

One of the many food stands scattered throughout the park.

Ever since the Phoenix opened at Knoebels, the park staff planned to eventually add another wooden roller coaster. For a number of years, the question was what kind of ride to build. They wanted it to complement the Phoenix, with its long, straight drops, and to be a traditional ride that would appeal to a wide variety of riders. In searching for an appropriate ride, they discovered the Mister Twister, in Denver, which had been abandoned in 1994 when Elitch Gardens relocated. Knoebels staff determined that the ride was not in suitable condition for relocation, but liked its twisting layout with its high-speed turns. They were able to obtain the original blueprints for the coaster and modified them to fit into Knoebels.

In 1999, the 3,900-foot-long, 102-foot-tall Twister opened in a previously undeveloped area of the park. The coaster has a 90-foot drop, a curved loading station, and due to site constraints, a double-lift hill in which the train travels 60 feet uphill, turns around, and travels up 42 more feet before plunging down.

Knoebels Today

Knoebels is considered the largest free-admission amusement park in the country today. While there are a variety of newer rides to enjoy, Knoebels has maintained its small-town charm, with huge trees shading a rambling layout of rides, games, and concessions. The park has forty-eight rides, fifteen of which are for children, a swimming pool, water slides, miniature golf, carousel and mining museums, a logging display, and a dozen shops.

From the park entrance, visitors access the expansive picnic groves and some of the park's newer rides, including the Giant Wheel, Sklooosh, bumper boats, and Power Surge, which replaced AXS in 2000. This leads to the oldest area of the park, home to the original swimming pool, Alamo restaurant, Grand Carousel, Roaring Creek Saloon, and Playland arcade.

To the right of this are a variety of older rides, including the Skooter bumper cars, Whipper, High Speed Thrill Coaster, Motor Boats, and Satellite. Beyond this area are most of the park's kiddie rides, along with the Stein and Goldstein carousel and Old Smoky train. To the left of the Grand Carousel, across Roaring Creek, are the miniature golf course, Whirlwind, Haunted Mansion, logging area, and carousel museum.

Many of the park's larger rides are located beyond this area, including the Phoenix, the Flume, and the Antique Autos. The Twister is located in the newest area of the park, between the Phoenix and the campground and pool.

Dutch Wonderland

OPENED 1963

ROUTE 30 EAST OF LANCASTER IN THE HEART OF PENNSYLVANIA DUTCH country is a typical tourist strip. Every year, 5 million visitors travel to this region, and most of them stop to take advantage of the motels, restaurants, and outlet stores congregated there. Among this jumble of businesses is a large castle containing a gift shop, with log-shaped boats carrying families in an adjacent pond, and a monorail whisking its passengers above the parking lot. Beyond the gift shop are a roller coaster and the gardens that make up the soul of Dutch Wonderland, a tranquil getaway a world away from the hustle and bustle of the tourist strip.

A Place for the Kids

Earl Clark was a potato broker from Lancaster County who traveled up and down the eastern seaboard buying potatoes for Pennsylvania potato chip factories. In 1958, tiring of the long periods on the road, Clark decided to settle down in Lancaster and construct a motel to serve the tourists flocking to the region. With fifty-two rooms, it was the largest motel in town, and people thought Clark was crazy to build such a large facility. But by 1959, he needed to add another twenty rooms. In 1961, Clark got an offer he couldn't refuse for the motel, and he decided to move onto bigger and better things.

During his years in the motel business, Clark noticed that visitors were constantly complaining about the lack of attractions for kids, and this was hurting business at his motel. "People would come in, stay one night, and leave," according to

Dutch Wonderland
2249 Route 30 East
Lancaster, PA 17602
717-291-1888
www.dutchwonderland.com

171

Dutch Wonderland, just before its 1963 opening. COLLECTION OF DUTCH WONDERLAND

his son Murl. Clark set out to fill this need and spent a year traveling around the country to amusement parks looking for ideas.

In late 1962, he began construction on a 14-acre site near his former motel. On May 20, 1963, Dutch Wonderland opened to the public. Fronting the highway, he built a large, castle-themed gift shop to attract attention and serve as an entrance to the new park. Clark wanted his park to be a true family attraction, with rides that the entire family could enjoy, a philosophy that guides Dutch Wonderland to this day. That first season, the park featured four rides: the Wonderland Special train, a half-mile-long ride around the entire park; the Lady Gay Riverboat, on the Old Mill Stream, which ran along the back of the park; the Turnpike car ride; and whale boats in a pond next to the castle. All of the rides are still in operation, although the whale boats were converted to log boats in 1975, and the train and Turnpike have been updated.

In addition to the gift shop and the rides, the park was filled with a wide array of smaller attractions, including a gingerbread house, a shoe slide, an Indian village, a space station, and a miniature Amish farm with a slide down the silo and a large fiberglass cow that kids could milk. Also scattered throughout the park were animated dioramas depicting Amish life, complete with authentic dialect. Most of these attractions are still enjoyed by visitors today.

LOCATION

Dutch Wonderland is located 4 miles east of Lancaster on U.S. Route 30.

OPERATING SCHEDULE

Dutch Wonderland is open daily from Memorial Day weekend through Labor Day, and weekends from mid-April through May and September through October. Opening time is 10 A.M. Closing time varies from 6 to 8:30 P.M., depending on the time of year.

ADMISSION

Parking is free, and a one-price admission for under $30 entitles you to enjoy all rides and attractions except the games and the monorail, which cost extra. Discounts are available for kids under six and for senior citizens.

FOOD

Dutch Wonderland has about ten food stands. Major facilities include the Castle Lake Patio Cafeteria, near the front entrance, with sandwiches, salads, hot dogs, burgers, and peanut butter and jelly sandwiches; Park Place, near the Old Mill Stream, serving roasted chicken, hot dogs, and burgers; and Rafters, next to the Pipeline Plunge. Stands throughout the park offer pretzels, popcorn, funnel cakes, pizza, and ice cream.

Although you are not permitted to bring food into the park, a picnic area is provided in the parking lot.

FOR CHILDREN

Dutch Wonderland was founded on the premise that families should be able to play together. As a result, only five rides have height restrictions, and kids taller than 42 inches can ride everything in the park. About a half dozen kiddie rides are scattered throughout the park, along with a variety of playground equipment.

SPECIAL FEATURES

Every year, Dutch Wonderland plants over one hundred thousand plants and flowers throughout the grounds. Most of the planting is done in the botanical garden, an attraction not found in most amusement parks.

Although the roller coasters here are not huge thrillers, they are quite fun, and each of them represents the first of its kind. The Sky Princess was the first project from Custom Coasters, now the world's largest builder of wooden roller coasters, and started a new era in which amusement parks around the world added family-size roller coasters. Joust was the first roller coaster made by Chance Manufacturing.

(continued on page 174)

VISITING (continued from page 173)

DUTCH WONDERLAND

TIME REQUIRED

If you have small kids, a visit to Dutch Wonderland can fill an entire day. If your time is limited, the major attractions can be enjoyed in about four hours.

TOURING TIPS

Try to visit during the week, when crowds tend to be lighter.

Dutch Wonderland offers a preview admission plan: If you pay full price three hours or less before closing, you receive a pass good for the whole next day.

The park is in the heart of Pennsylvania Dutch Country, so it can be part of a larger vacation.

Another attraction built the first year was a modest shack along the banks of Old Mill Stream. This Hobo Shack was built as tribute to one of Clark's favorite entertainers, Red Skelton, and his character Freddie the Freeloader. It remains at the park and was even visited by Skelton in 1975.

Clark loved flowers, and he filled the park with thousands of colorful plantings, a tradition that continues to this day. In the early years, tight funds did not permit the installation of an irrigation system, so Earl and his oldest son, Murl, moved hoses around at night to water the plants.

During its second season, in 1964, Dutch Wonderland added one of its most unusual attractions, the Dutch Wonder House. This is a modern

The whale boats and the Castle Gift Shop were two of Dutch Wonderland's original features. AUTHOR'S COLLECTION

One hundred thousand plants adorn the 5-acre botanical garden.

adaptation of a classic illusion ride that was popular in the early 1900s. The ride creates the feeling that you are being flipped upside down.

By 1966, business had grown to the point that Dutch Wonderland was able to purchase an adjacent farm and undertake a major expansion. A portion of the acreage was developed into the Old Mill Stream Campground, and much of the remaining acreage was developed into a 5-acre botanical garden. Located at the back of the park, across the Old Mill Stream from the rest of the park, the garden contains nearly one hundred thousand flowers and shrubs planted in an around-the-world theme. The gardens were adorned with miniature replicas of the Leaning Tower of Pisa, the Eiffel Tower, Big Ben, a Swiss chalet, a Japanese pagoda, a Hawaiian hut, and a Dutch windmill, which was converted into a Ferris wheel in 1982. In the center of the gardens was the Clark tower, a colorful, 24-foot tower topped by an American flag. A series of canals were dug through the gardens for a gondola boat ride.

But while the campground and botanical garden were indeed major additions, what really caught everyone's attention that year was the construction of a large monorail ride. The mile-long track had two five-car trains that traveled above the park and parking lot along U.S. Route 30. Besides the station in the park, there was a second station in the parking lot so that visitors could enjoy the ride and see Dutch Wonderland without paying admission. Given that Disneyland's monorail had opened just

The Double Splash Flume is just the right size for the entire family to enjoy.

seven years earlier, the fact that a small, three-year-old park had added such a ride created a sensation. "It really put the park on the map," recalls Murl Clark.

Growth continued with the addition in 1967 of a sky ride traversing the park and a tugboat ride in the Old Mill Stream, and in 1968 a giant slide in response to the giant slide craze sweeping America at the time. Rebuilt in 1987, it remains one of the last giant slides in operation.

The 1970s began with the installation of a traditional amusement park favorite, bumper cars. But as with many Pennsylvania amusement parks in 1972, the park was flooded when Hurricane Agnes caused the Old Mill Stream to overflow its banks. The park had $160,000 in damages, but it recovered quickly, and more family attractions were added. In 1974, the Old 99 train ride was given a prominent location in the middle of the park, between the Wonderland Special train and the Turnpike ride, and 1975 saw the addition of a miniature animated circus, with five thousand handcrafted characters.

By the late 1970s, log flume rides had become a favorite family attraction at amusement parks around the world. Dutch Wonderland's owners knew that one would fit perfectly at their park and contracted with Arrow Dynamics, the leading manufacturer of log flumes in the 1970s, to build one. Given the family orientation of the park, Dutch Wonderland's flume, at 807 feet long, was smaller than the rides at larger theme parks, but it featured two splash-down drops of 25 and 12 feet. Dutch Wonderland's ride has multicolored logs, rather than the traditional brown ones.

Dutch Wonderland was once again flooded on January 23, 1978, as heavy rains melted accumulated snow and caused the Old Mill Stream to rise. The botanical garden was inundated, the Riverboat was washed a mile and a half downstream, the Indian village was destroyed, and many picnic tables were swept away.

But again Dutch Wonderland quickly bounced back and soon added an Astroliner ride. The Astroliner was a new concept in which riders entered a large rocket for a simulated trip into outer space. An operator aboard the rocket controlled the movements of the rocket with a joystick. Dutch Wonderland was one of the first parks to add such an attraction.

The 1980s marked continued growth for Dutch Wonderland, with the addition of attractions such as a diving show in 1980, a merry-go-round in 1981, the Space Shuttle swinging ride in 1984, and the Flying Trapeze in 1986. The decade also saw two major fires. The first, in 1985, caused $1 million in damage to the gift shop; the second, in 1989, destroyed one of the monorail stations and two of its three trains, shutting down the ride for the rest of the year. But the park soon recovered, and it entered the 1990s stronger than ever.

A Roller Coaster Decade

Dutch Wonderland's target audience, kids under the age of thirteen, had changed since the park opened in 1963. Not only were they more sophisticated, but they were more daring, and the park decided that a roller coaster should be added to the lineup. Although they briefly considered adding a small steel-track ride, they thought that the look and sound of a wooden roller coaster would be more popular with the families that flocked to the park. In the early 1990s, however, the few wooden roller coasters being built tended to be large rides at major theme parks. But Dutch Wonderland was intrigued by the prospect of a smaller wooden roller coaster and found a new company, Custom Coasters, that was willing to build one. It was the first project for what is today the largest wooden roller coaster manufacturer in the world.

In 1992, the Sky Princess, a new $1.75 million wooden roller coaster, was ready for passengers. It is a true family ride, standing 55 feet tall and 1,700 feet long, with a top speed of 40 miles per hour. To make it more visually exciting, the L-shaped ride was built around the flume, and the monorail track runs through and above the structure.

Like the monorail twenty-six years earlier, the Sky Princess took Dutch Wonderland to a whole new level. To accommodate the increasing

Sky Princess kicked off a new era of development of medium-size wooden roller coasters.

crowds, Dutch Wonderland opened a new area in 1996 on 4 acres of undeveloped land. This increased the total park size to 48 acres, more than triple the acreage when the park opened thirty-three years earlier.

Anchoring the new area was the Pipeline Plunge water coaster, a $900,000 water slide ride. The Pipeline Plunge was joined by new food concessions and games, and a relocated Flying Trapeze ride. The Sky Princess and the Pipeline Plunge were both visible from Route 30, helping attract passersby.

Given the success of the Sky Princess, Dutch Wonderland decided to add a second roller coaster in 1998, this one a steel-track ride. The park wanted something to appeal to guests too small to enjoy the Sky Princess. At that time, Chance Manufacturing, a successful builder of spinning rides, including Dutch Wonderland's Space Shuttle, Flying Trapeze, and merry-go-round rides, was developing its first roller coaster, and Dutch Wonderland was at the front of the line to purchase one. Named Joust, at 17 feet high and 350 feet long, the park knew it would be the perfect complement to Sky Princess and set it up right next door.

In an increasingly sophisticated world, the Astroliner was starting to show its age, and in 2000, Dutch Wonderland purchased a new simulator ride, the VR Voyager. Unlike the Astroliner, the ride was totally computer controlled and could play any one of fifteen different movies. But when the park could not locate a buyer for the Astroliner, they decided to keep it and allow visitors to experience both the oldest and newest examples of ride simulator technology. The two simulators sit side by side in the renovated Space Station area, which now carries broadcasts from the Kennedy and Johnson Space Centers.

In 2001, after building the park into one of central Pennsylvania's leading attractions, the Clark family decided to sell Dutch Wonderland to the Hershey Entertainment and Resort Company, the owner of nearby Hersheypark.

Dutch Wonderland Today

Over the years, Dutch Wonderland has evolved from a small roadside tourist attraction into a major amusement park. Its tree-shaded grounds and intricate landscaping provide a peaceful contrast to the bustling tourist strip just outside its gates. From its original four rides, the park now features nearly thirty rides, live shows, and numerous smaller attractions scattered throughout the grounds. Dutch Wonderland continues to embrace founder Earl Clark's vision, as most attractions can be enjoyed by the entire family.

Visitors enter through the Castle Gift Shop, which leads straight to the heart of the park, where it all started. Among the rides found in this area are the Wonderland Special train, log boats, Sky Ride, Old 99 train, Turnpike, and Monorail. Beyond this area are many of the park's newer attractions, including the bumper cars, merry-go-round, and roller coasters—Joust and Sky Princess—along with the diving show and miniature circus. Along the Old Mill Stream are the Indian village, the Dutch Wonder House, and the Riverboat and tugboat rides.

At the back of the park are the botanical gardens, 5 acres with one hundred thousand plants and miniature replicas of international landmarks. A gondola boat provides a tour of the gardens.

Dutch Wonderland is a great place to bring the camera, as there are lots of picture-taking opportunities throughout park, with things such as oversize pretzels, giant chairs, and fiberglass farm animals for kids to climb on, as well as a miniature church and a one-room schoolhouse where kids can ring the bell.

PENNSYLVANIA

Sesame Place

OPENED 1981

ON FIRST GLANCE, LANGHORNE, JUST NORTH OF PHILADELPHIA, LOOKS like typical suburbia, dominated by malls and signs beckoning passing motorists to stores. But you know that something special is going on here when you see the town water tower adorned with Bert, Ernie, the Cookie Monster, and other characters from the children's television show "Sesame Street."

A Different Kind of Theme Park

In the mid-1970s, the Children's Television Workshop, producers of the renowned educational shows "Sesame Street" and "The Electric Company," began researching ways to bring their theories on childhood development directly to kids and their families. Over a three-year period, they developed a concept for a theme park that, rather than traditional rides, emphasized interactive activities. Lacking theme park development expertise, they formed a partnership with Busch Entertainment, which owned Busch Gardens in Florida and Virginia, and was one of the most successful and experienced theme park operators in the country.

On June 26, 1979, ground was broken on a 15-acre site north of Philadelphia, and just over a year later, the $9 million attraction was ready for the public. Visitors found a theme park unlike any ever constructed before. Guests entered through a large replica of Big Bird's head, which led to a suspension bridge that took them into the park. Attractions were spread over 3.5 acres and were divided into three areas: the Land Court, the

Sesame Place
100 Sesame Rd.
P.O. Box L579
Langhorne, PA 19047
215-752-7070
www.sesameplace.com

180

Water Court, and the Air Court. The Land Court was dominated by Nets and Climbs, a giant climbing structure, standing 40 feet high, with a series of nets and slides. Other attractions included Cookie Mountain, a climbing activity; Monster Maze, a forest of punching bags; Ernie's Bed Bounce, a giant mattress for kids to jump on; and the Construction Company, with oversize building blocks. The Water Court's main feature was the Count's Ballroom, a "pool" of eighty thousand colored balls on a trampoline surface. Other attractions included the Amazing Mumford's Water Maze, Bert's Balancing Beams, and Sesame Beach, a giant sandbox. The Air Court was home to the Rainbow Pyramid, where kids could suspend balls on jets of air.

In addition to the three courts, the park featured Sesame Studio, with forty different science activities, and the Computer Gallery, which had sixty-seven games. Even the Food Factory was designed to develop young minds, with food preparation areas visible to the public. Unlike many child-oriented parks, Sesame Place tried to include parents wherever possible, with sixteen of the forty outdoor play elements open to adults.

This "playground of the twenty-first century" was an immediate sensation. Large crowds of up to twelve thousand caused the gates to be closed on twenty-five days in its first month of operation, and by the end of the first season, more than three hundred thousand people had gone through the gates. Sesame Place was a winner.

Nets and Climbs and Amazing Mumford's Water Maze are two of Sesame Place's original attractions.

Big Bird's Rambling River anchors the Sesame Island section. PHOTO BY SESAME PLACE

Getting Bigger

The next few seasons focused on expanding existing attractions to accommodate the growing crowds. In 1983, Sesame Place added several new attractions, including a live show with Sesame Street characters; Little Bird's Court, an activity area for small children; and 200 feet of tunnels, 20 to 35 feet above the ground, in Nets and Climbs. But most significant was the construction of two water slides: the 130-foot-long Zoom Flume and Slippery Slope, a 75-foot-long slide dropping into a large pool.

The water slides were soon the most popular activity in the park, and over the next three years, Sesame Place concentrated on water-oriented attractions, such as the 350-foot-long Runaway Rapids and 150-foot-long Rubber Duckie Rapids in 1984; the Big Slipper double water slide and Count's Fount water play area in 1985; and Sesame Streak, a 300-foot-long double water slide in 1986. Also that year, the Big Bird Theater was built for the increasingly popular Sesame Street character show.

In 1988, Sesame Place built a full-scale replica of Sesame Street, where guests could visit with their favorite characters and play at Mr. MacIntosh's Fruit Stand and Engine House No. 1. The original park was bursting at the seams, and as a result, Sesame Place kicked off the 1990s by developing a portion of its old parking lot into a new 2.5-acre area—Sesame Island. The main attraction in this Caribbean-themed area is

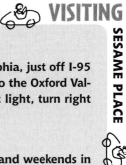

LOCATION

Sesame Place is located about thirty minutes north of Philadelphia, just off I-95 and U.S. Route 1. From I-95, take Exit 46 onto Route 1 North to the Oxford Valley exit. Turn right on Oxford Valley Road. At the third traffic light, turn right into Sesame Place.

OPERATING SCHEDULE

Sesame Place is open daily from mid-May through Labor Day and weekends in September and October. Operating times vary, depending on the time of year.

ADMISSION

Pay-one-price admission for under $40 entitles you to enjoy all rides, shows, and attractions. Parking costs extra.

FOOD

More than a dozen food facilities are scattered throughout the park, ranging from portable carts to cafeteria-style eateries with an emphasis on nutritious foods. Food Factory, in the center of the park, is the largest facility and the only one with indoor seating. It serves freshly prepared pizza, sandwiches, salads, and desserts. Captain Ernie's Café in Sesame Island has turkey sandwiches, burgers, salads, and desserts. Stands and carts offer hot dogs, pretzels, nachos, ice cream, and beverages.

Special kids' meals are available at Food Factory, Captain Ernie's Café, and Sesame Sandwich Shop next to Count's Fount.

You may bring food into the park. Picnic areas are located near Nets and Climbs and in Sesame Island.

FOR CHILDREN

Sesame Place is designed for kids between three and thirteen, and all of the activities have been built with them in mind.

SPECIAL FEATURES

Sesame Place is the only theme park in the Unites States where you can meet characters from Sesame Street.

TIME REQUIRED

If you have young kids, Sesame Place can easily fill an entire day, with the participatory activities, water attractions, and shows.

TOURING TIPS

Try to visit on a weekday, particularly Monday or Tuesday, as they tend to be less crowded.

Enjoy the water activities early or late in the day, as they are most crowded in the middle of the day when it is hottest.

(continued on page 184)

VISITING (continued from page 183)

SESAME PLACE

> The peak time for lunch is between 12 and 2 P.M. Try to plan your eating schedule around this.
>
> Bring aqua shoes, as it makes getting around the park in swimsuits easier.
>
> Lockers are available near the front entrance and next to Count's Fount and can be rented for the entire day.

Big Bird's Rambling River, a 1,000-foot-long river on which kids and their parents ride inner tubes through geysers and a mist-filled tunnel. Other attractions include Ernie's Waterworks, a water play area; Oscar's Trash Can Bandstand, with real steel drums for kids to play; Sandcastle Beach; and an 800-seat theater.

Much of the remaining original parking lot was redeveloped in 1993 into the 1.5-acre Twiddlebugland. A salute to Twiddlebugs, the friendly insects that reside in Ernie and Bert's window box and collect lost and discarded objects, the area is designed to help children learn about recycling. Throughout Twiddlebugland are oversize items scaled so that a 4-foot-tall child would be the same size as an adult Twiddlebug. The giant items include a bucket and spoon that kids can slide down, marbles to climb on, a garden hose squirting water, and a record turntable. The main attraction is Teeny Tiny Tidal Wave, a 10,000-square-foot wave pool, flanked by smaller wading pools. Overseeing the activity in the pool is a 16-foot cutout of Ernie's head. Twiddlebugland also features

The Vapor Trail was added to Sesame Place in 1998.

Sesame Place's first traditional ride—Mix 'n' Match Twiddle Tracks, kid-powered handcars that look like miniature matchboxes.

A parade traveling through the heart of the park made its debut in 1994, and Twiddlebugland saw the addition of the park's largest water slide, Sky Splash, in 1995. Topped by an 8-foot-tall rubber duckie sitting in a giant soapdish, the 50-foot-tall slide has huge inner tubes that fit six people, allowing the entire family to slide together. The next year saw the addition of Slimey's Chutes, a double water slide named for Oscar the Grouch's pet worm, Slimey.

Sesame Place took a whole new direction in 1998 with the addition of Vapor Trail, a family-size steel-track roller coaster. Built in response to the growing popularity of roller coasters, the 1,300-foot-long, 56-foot-tall Vapor Trail dominates the front entrance to the park and relies on fast turns rather than big drops for thrills. Riders enter through Super Grover's phone booth, which leads to the space station boarding platform, where they board rocket-shaped cars to join Grover in a race through the solar system.

Sesame Place Today

Today Sesame Place maintains its original emphasis on participatory attractions, with over fifty kid-powered activities, but it has grown to include fifteen water attractions and two traditional rides. Just past the front entrance is a wide boulevard that divides the park. To the right is the Vapor Trail roller coaster, along with Sesame Place's original attractions, including most of the climbing activities; Sesame Studio; the Games Gallery; and Mr. Hooper's Emporium, the main gift shop. The area also has a variety of water attractions, including most of those for smaller kids, such as Little Bird's Birdbath, Rubber Duckie Pond, and Count's Fount. Sesame Street is located at the end of the main boulevard and is the place to meet all of your children's favorite Sesame Street characters.

To the left of the main boulevard are Sesame Place's two newest areas: Twiddlebugland and Sesame Island. Twiddlebugland, located closest to the front of the park, is home to Sky Splash, the park's largest water attraction, along with Teeny Tiny Tidal Wave and Slimey's Chutes. Sesame Island is home to Big Bird's Rambling River and Ernie's Waterworks.

The park also features approximately a half dozen live shows. The parade takes place on the main boulevard and features all of the Sesame Street characters. Other shows take place in the Circle Theater, next to Nets and Climbs; at the Big Bird Theater, in the back of the park at the end of the main boulevard; at the Paradise Theater, in Sesame Island; and in Sesame Studio.

Pennsylvania's Smaller Parks

ONE OF THE WONDERFUL CHARACTERISTICS OF PENNSYLVANIA'S amusement park industry is that in addition to the wealth of larger parks, there are also a variety of smaller ones. Though these parks may not be large enough for a full day's outing, they are well worth a stop if you're in the area. The following sections profile some of Pennsylvania's most interesting smaller amusement parks.

PEN ARGYL

Weona Park

OPENED 1920

Weona Park, with its tree-shaded grounds, picnic pavilions, swimming pool, playground, miniature golf course, and rides, is reminiscent of the dozens of small country amusement parks that once dotted Pennsylvania. Weona Park is a true community park that came into existence due to the complete participation of the citizens of Pen Argyl, a town of three thousand located among the slate quarries of eastern Pennsylvania.

In 1919, the town banded together to purchase a 17-acre tract on the eastern edge of town with a combination of public funds, private donations, corporate gifts, and money raised by sell-

Weona Park
P.O. Box 335
Pen Argyl, PA 18072
610-863-9249
www.pahs.org/OurTown/
carousel.html

ing shares to the public. The entire town, from business executives to quarry workers, labored during the summer of 1920 to reclaim the swampy land and create a community gathering place. A naming contest was then held, and the name Weona ("We own a") Park was chosen as a tribute to the citizens of Pen Argyl. Initially the park contained little more than an athletic field, but soon the town added a swimming pool and bathhouse.

Seeking something truly special for the park, the town decided to purchase a carousel. Funding would not permit the acquisition of one of the huge, elaborate machines that were all the rage at that time. As a result, Pen Argyl contracted with well-known carousel manufacturer William Dentzel of Germantown, a Philadelphia neighborhood, to create a carousel that would suit the town's limited budget.

During the 1920s, it was common for larger amusement parks to trade in their older carousels for newer models that featured more elaborate carvings and animals that moved up and down. As a result, most manufacturers had a large inventory of old carousels and animals to draw from. Dentzel took an old carousel frame from one of these trade-ins and populated it with surplus animals that had also been traded in, thereby creating a gem of a machine for Weona Park. The carousel fea-

Weona Park is reminiscent of the dozens of "country" amusement parks that used to dot Pennsylvania.

Weona Park is located on the east side of Pen Argyl on PA Route 512. The park features two rides, miniature golf, a swimming pool, and picnic facilities. Admission is free, and all attractions are pay-as-you-go. The rides are open weekends from Memorial Day to Labor Day.

tures forty-four animals, all hand carved between 1885 and 1917—thirty-four horses, three giraffes, three goats, three deer, and one zebra—along with two chariots. A building was constructed at the front of the park to house the ride, which opened in 1923.

Over the decades, other features were added at Weona Park. A miniature golf course was constructed in 1935, a ballroom was built in 1956, and several kiddie rides, including a train, small Ferris wheel, and jeep ride, were added in the early 1960s.

As times changed, so did the park. The train was removed in the 1980s, and the Ferris wheel was sold in 2000. But Weona Park remains a beloved community institution. A local citizen restored the jeep ride in 1997, and an area teenager renovated the miniature golf course in 2000 as his Eagle Scout project.

The largest project was a restoration of the carousel. Since its 1923 debut, the carousel had given hundreds of thousands of rides, and by the 1990s, it was beginning to show its age. Though the animal bodies had held up well, years of varnish and touch-up paint had obscured many of the animals' details. The community once again came together to fund the restoration effort, and starting in 1997, each animal was removed from the carousel and sent to carousel artist Lisa Parr for restoration. She carefully removed the layers of yellowed varnish and recent touch-ups to expose the original paint, repainted any bare spots, and applied a new coat of varnish. All of the animals were completed by 2000, restoring the ride to the way it appeared when it debuted at the park in 1923. It is one of only three carousels in the country that still feature their original paint. In 1999, the carousel was added to the National Register of Historic Places.

Plans are under way to restore the carousel building and to purchase a band organ to provide music for the ride, much like its original band organ did from the 1930s through the 1960s.

Over the years, Weona Park has persevered. It remains a charming reminder of the little amusement parks that once existed on the outskirts of so many Pennsylvania towns.

BARTONSVILLE

PENNSYLVANIA

Pocono Play Park
OPENED 1970

The story of Pocono Play Park does not begin in Pennsylvania, but in Bayonne, New Jersey, at a long-gone amusement park known as Uncle Milty's. From the mid-1950s through the early 1970s, Uncle Milty's enticed the youth of New Jersey to the foot of the Bayonne Bridge. One of these kids was Joe Pandolfo, and his many visits to the park ignited a dream that would be fulfilled in 1995 when he purchased Pocono Putter, a small entertainment center in the heart of the Pocono Mountain tourist belt.

Opened in 1970, Pocono Putter was a modest roadside facility along a stretch of restaurants and outlet stores and featured little more than a miniature golf course, a driving range, and batting cages. But Pandolfo saw potential for the little park, which he renamed Pocono Play Park,

Pocono Play Park
Route 611
Bartonsville, PA 18321
570-920-0820
www.poconogokart.com

and in the summer of 1995, he launched an expansion program that included the installation of two go-cart tracks—one for kids and one for adults. Bumper cars joined the lineup in 1996.

Remembering the rides he enjoyed in his youth, Pandolfo next added several traditional amusement park rides. Three classic kiddie rides—a roto whip, a Ferris wheel, and a pony cart—were added next to the miniature golf course in 1997. A kiddie roller coaster and kiddie car ride replaced the kiddie Ferris wheel in 1999. The park now has a total of eight rides.

Given that much of the appeal of the Poconos lies in its wealth of activities for sports enthusiasts, Pocono Play Park took a new direction in 2000 with the addition of a sports area, which features two paintball battlefields, a basketball-shooting course, a skate park, a paintball shooting gallery, and an archery shooting range.

VISITING

POCONO PLAY PARK

Pocono Play Park is located on PA Route 611, about 1.5 miles west of Exit 302B of I-80 (turn left at the light). The park is open daily Memorial Day through Labor Day and on weekends only in April, May, September, October, and November. Several sports activities are open through the winter, weather permitting. During October, Pocono Play Park offers pumpkin picking and a hayride. Admission to the park is free, and all activities are priced individually.

Land of Little Horses
OPENED 1971

Tony Garulo traveled the world with the merchant marine. During a voyage to South America in the late 1960s, he came across an article in *Life* magazine about a breed of miniature horses raised since the mid-1800s by the Falabella family in Argentina. He became enchanted with the 3-foot-tall animals and was able to visit the Falabella farm during a stop at Buenos Aires.

> **Land of Little Horses**
> 125 Glenwood Dr.
> Gettysburg, PA 17325
> 717-334-7259
> www.landoflittlehorses.com

After he retired from the merchant marine, Garulo wanted to make the miniature horses his full-time occupation. He purchased a 100-acre farm just west of Gettysburg and in 1971 opened the Gettysburg Miniature Horse Farm, with two dozen miniature horses. In the early years, one hundred thousand plus people visited the park to enjoy horse shows, a nature trail with animal displays, and pony rides.

In 1980, Garulo changed the name of the farm to Land of Little Horses. After he died in 1985, control of the facility fell into the hands of absentee owners, who let it run down. Land of Little Horses was on the brink of closing in 1993, when the Hawkins family purchased it and began renovating and expanding the park.

The first major addition that the Hawkinses constructed was a museum to display a collection of horse-drawn carriages. The following year, they added a tram ride that takes visitors through the park's heavily wooded nature area, past displays of more than three hundred animals, including Barbados sheep, Sicilian donkeys, ostriches, llamas, four different kinds of goats, and five types of pheasants.

In 1996, they purchased a merry-go-round intended to commemorate the Falabella horses. Originally manufactured in 1929, it is one of the earliest examples of a portable carnival-style merry-go-round and was

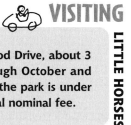 **VISITING**

LITTLE HORSES

Land of Little Horses is just south of U.S. Route 30, on Glenwood Drive, about 3 miles west of Gettysburg. The park is open daily April through October and weekends from Thanksgiving through Christmas. Admission to the park is under $10 and includes all shows and displays. Rides are an additional nominal fee.

PENNSYLVANIA

one of the first to feature aluminum horses. The ride even made an appearance at the 1939 New York World's Fair. The park also features a miniature pony cart ride, horse shows, and pig races.

MANSFIELD

Bucktail Family Fun Park and Camping Resort
OPENED 1986

Bucktail Family Fun Park and Camping Resort came about by accident. In 1985, Richard Franks, a real estate developer, was presented with an opportunity to purchase a 350-acre tract of land near Mansfield, Pennsylvania, in the far north-central reaches of the state. The property had one drawback—it contained a run-down campground. Initially Franks resisted, but not wanting to lose out on the entire land parcel, he reluctantly entered the campground business. Although he undertook only minor improvements his first season, he was able to increase revenues sixfold. Franks realized that the campground, which he had initially planned to convert to other uses, had great potential.

"Given the remote location of Bucktail Camping Resort, we knew we had to come up with a hook," recalls Franks. "It occurred to me that there was not much for kids in this business. So why not make them our hook?" One of the first things he did was add a miniature golf course, which has continued to expand and now has twenty-one holes. Wanting to add other child-oriented activities, Franks knew there were few activities that kids love more than amusement rides.

He eventually came into contact with George Perluke, who had been stockpiling rides in the northeastern Pennsylvania town of Berwick for an amusement park that never came to be. When he first saw the rides, Frank was immediately drawn to a miniature railroad locomotive sitting forlornly in the weeds. He knew it would be the perfect addition for his fledgling operation, so he purchased it and immediately began restoration.

Bucktail Family Fun Park and Camping Resort
1029 Mann Creek Rd.
Mansfield, PA 16933
570-662-2923
www.bucktailcamping.com

This locomotive was a true piece of history. It was built in 1928 by the Industrial Railway Locomotive Works of New York City, a company formed to develop gasoline-powered locomotives, rather than the steam-driven trains that were common

Bucktail Family Fun Park and Camping Resort is located just outside Mansfield on Mann Creek Road. From U.S. Route 15, proceed .25 mile east on Route 6 to Lambs Creek Road. Turn left (north), and go 1.5 miles north to Mann Creek Road. Turn left and drive 1 mile. Once you get off Route 15, the route to the park is marked by signs featuring park mascot Bucky. The campground is open from mid-April through the end of October. Admission to the park and all activities are free to campground guests. Unlimited activities are available to day visitors for a small fee (under $10). Bucktail presents special events almost every weekend throughout the season.

during the era. But because of the Depression and design problems, the company built only six locomotives. Bucktail's is the last one known in existence.

After a year of restoration work, construction, and lots of TLC, the Bucktail and Western Railroad opened on Memorial Day 1987, providing rides through the thick woods that surrounded the campground. But while the train was a popular addition to the campground, its Ford Model A automobile engine made it an operational headache. As a result, Franks bought two more used trains, produced by the Miniature Rail-

Bucktail Camping Resort's original train ride remains on display.

road Company of Rensselaer, Indiana, the leading manufacturer of amusement park trains during the 1940s and 1950s. Restoration of the new trains was completed in 1994, and the original locomotive was retired, although it remains on display.

In 1986, Franks had stumbled across another classic amusement park ride at Lenape Park, in West Chester, Pennsylvania, which had closed and was selling its rides—the Venetian Swing ride, which had been added to Lenape Park around 1918. This is a simple ride in which two people sit in a boatlike swing suspended from a large A-frame and pull on a rope to swing back and forth. Bucktail's is one of the last surviving examples of what was once a very common ride.

By now, the park had established itself in the market and had become a successful growing operation. The ride lineup was expanded in 1990 with the addition of a kiddie handcar ride, and in 1992 Franks restored a genuine 1952 fire truck to give rides around the grounds.

But he felt that something was still missing—no amusement park was complete without a merry-go-round. Franks found a carnival owner trying to sell the frame of an old merry-go-round. Manufactured around 1914 by the Allan Herschell Company of North Tonawanda, New York, and originally owned by a fire department in Maryland, the ride was in sad shape by the time Franks discovered it. All of the original wooden horses had been sold, and most of the parts needed to be totally rebuilt. But Franks viewed it as an opportunity to do something special. After extensively renovating the framework, he purchased aluminum merry-go-round animals and asked friends and campers to paint and name them. The merry-go-round was put in a prominent location and in 1993 opened to enthusiastic crowds.

The attraction lineup has continued to grow. In 1996, an enclosed pit filled with twenty-seven thousand colored balls was added, and Willy the Worm, a kiddie train ride consisting of a tractor pulling a train of apple juice barrels, joined the park in 1997. In 2001, a spiraling Helter Skelter Slide and a Moonwalk were added. The park now features a total of eight rides, a swimming pool, playground, game room, and miniature golf course.

Carousel Village at Indian Walk

OPENED 1992

One always has to be careful at auctions; you never know what you might buy. For Sam Willard, a spur-of-the-moment bid at an auction was his ticket to owning his own amusement park.

Sam Willard has operated Indian Walk Farm, a Christmas tree farm and garden center in Wrightstown, about 25 miles north of Philadelphia, since 1962. In the late 1980s, he decided to convert an old barn on the property into a series of craft and antique shops.

While searching for memorabilia to decorate the shops, Willard found himself at an auction in East Hampton, New Jersey, at the winter home of the Wallendas of high-wire fame. The Wallendas' winter quarters are located on the former site of Butler Park, an amusement park that closed in the 1950s. In addition to lots of circus memorabilia, the auction featured the last relic of the property's amusement park era—a carousel, long since stripped of its horses.

> **Carousel Village at Indian Walk**
> Route 413
> Wrightstown, PA 18940
> 215-598-0202

Given the deteriorated state of the ride, the auctioneer was having a tough time attracting bids and asked Willard, a longtime friend, to bid $1,000 on the broken-down machine to help get the bidding started. No other bids were made, however, and Willard found himself the owner of a run-down carousel with no horses.

Even though he could have written off the expense and scrapped the ride, there was something about it that appealed to Willard. The ride

VISITING

Carousel Village at Indian Walk is located on PA Route 413 in Wrightstown, 25 miles north of Philadelphia. From the Pennsylvania Turnpike (I-276), take Exit 351, and go north on U.S. Route 1 to PA Route 413 North through Newtown. The rides operate from April through December, weather permitting. The garden center and specialty shops are open year-round. Admission to the park is free, and all activities are pay-as-you-go.

Carousel Village's lovingly restored carousel enjoys a prominent location in the park.

was built sometime between 1891 and 1915 by the Herschell Spillman Company of North Tonawanda, New York, and was mounted on a circus wagon. Willard learned that only a few of these models had been manufactured, and this was the last one left. After traveling with carnivals in New Jersey during the early 1900s, it had found a home at Butler Park in 1926. It could not be determined what happened to the original horses. Willard wanted to keep it authentic, so he began going to auctions looking for Herschell Spillman horses. After acquiring twenty-four originals, he was anxious to return the ride to operation, so he hired a local artisan to create the final twelve animals. The new horses were carved as Indian ponies to pay homage to the Native American tribes that once populated the area. In addition, the ride was adorned with Native American pictures and panels representing the fourteen tribes that once inhabited the region.

Work was completed on the carousel in time to put it in operation in the garden center's front lawn for Indian Walk's annual Christmas festival in 1991. Today the carousel is the focal point of the entire complex, sitting front and center and surrounded by thousands of colorful flowers.

The carousel's successful debut encouraged Willard to continue adding rides, the first of which was a miniature train in 1993. Dubbed the Pine Needle Express, the new train provided a half-mile ride through the Christmas tree farm. Riders were taken past a collection of live animals from around the world, including familiar ones, such as sheep, goats, ostriches, and llamas, as well as unusual ones, such as highland steer and fallow deer. During the Christmas season, the train provides transportation from the parking lots to the Christmas tree farm, where visitors can pick out their own trees. The train also travels through a building featuring forty animated characters, whose theme changes with the holidays.

In 1994, Willard discovered two classic kiddie rides being sold by a nearby amusement park, Marty's Circus of Fun—fire engines and pony carts, originally manufactured in the 1920s by the W. F. Mangels Company of Coney Island, New York. He added an auto ride, featuring gasoline-powered antique car replicas, two years later.

In 1999, former major leaguer Steve Frey opened the Baseball Emporium, which offers baseball instruction. At Halloween, the Baseball Emporium is turned into a haunted house.

In 2000, a Red Baron kiddie ride was added, followed by a Little Dipper kiddie roller coaster in 2001. Features planned for the future include a Ferris wheel and miniature golf course.

Other Amusement Facilities

- *Albion Boro Park,* 15 Smock Avenue, Albion. Not an amusement park, but this municipal park is home to what is believed to be the third-oldest operating carousel in America, manufactured in the 1890s by the U.S. Merry-Go-Round Company. 814-756-3660

- *All Star Family Fun and Sports Complex,* Business Route 15, Gettysburg. Indoor-outdoor entertainment complex featuring two go-cart tracks, paddle boats, kiddie playground, kiddie cars, simulator ride, two miniature golf courses, and driving range. 717-334-6363. www.allstarpa.com.

- *Caddie Shak,* PA Route 31 East, Donegal. Home to three go-cart tracks, including one for kids, bumper boats, three kiddie rides, miniature golf, driving range, and paintball. 724-593-740. www.caddie shak.com.

- *Camelbeach,* Exit 299 off I-80, Tannersville. Water park featuring eight water slides, adventure river, family activity pool, and the largest wave pool in Pennsylvania. Camelbeach also has bumper boats, chairlift ride, alpine slide, and miniature golf. 570-629-1661. www.camelbeach.com.

- *City Island,* Market Street, Harrisburg. Large city park located on an island in the Susquehanna River. Numerous attractions include a boat ride in the river, 4,400-foot-long train ride, and antique kiddie carousel. 717-255-3020. www.harrisburgevents.com/cityisland/.

- *Dandy's Frontier Fun Park,* Route 322, Cranberry. Features two go-cart tracks, including one for kids, bumper boats, miniature golf, and batting cages. 814-677-5278.

- *Golf Park Plus,* Golf Park Drive, Hamlin. Features go-carts, bumper boats, scenic train ride, two miniature golf courses, paintball, and driving range. 570-689-4996. www.golfparkplus.com.

- *Happy Tymes Family Fun Center,* 2071 West County Line Road, Warrington. Indoor-outdoor facility with go-cart track, miniature golf, three kiddie rides, kids' play area, and batting cages. 215-343-6500.

- *Peddler's Village,* U.S. Route 202 and PA Route 263, Lahaska. Shopping village that includes a carousel museum and a carousel assembled using the mechanism from a 1922 Philadelphia Toboggan Company carousel and new hand-carved wooden horses. 215-794-4000. www.peddlersvillage.com

- *Pittsburgh Zoo and Aquarium,* One Wild Place, Pittsburgh. World-class zoo with merry-go-round, train, tram, and three kiddie rides. 412-665-3640; 800-474-4ZOO. www.pittsburghzoo.com.

- *Sandcastle,* 1000 Sandcastle Drive, West Homestead. Largest water park in Pennsylvania, with fifteen water slides, river ride, wave pool, kids' water area, "world's largest" hot tub, and go-carts. 412-462-6666. www.sandcastlewaterpark.com.

- *Shawnee Place,* off U.S. Route 209, Shawnee-on-Delaware. Play and water park for children under twelve and their families. Park features fifteen outdoor play activities, one kiddie ride, two water slides, and an activity pool. 570-421-7231. www.shawneemt.com.

- *Wet 'n' Wild Acres,* PA Route 36, Cooksburg. Located near Cook Forest State Park, this facility features two go-cart tracks, including one for kids, bumper boats, three kiddie rides, miniature golf, water slides, miniature golf, horse and pony rides, and petting zoo. 814-752-2600.

- *Wildwood Highlands,* 2330 Wildwood Road, Wildwood. Family entertainment center featuring go-carts, bumper boats, merry-go-round, three kiddie rides, kids' play area, two miniature golf courses, driving range, and laser tag. 412-487-5517. www.wildwoodpa.com.

- *World of Mazes,* Mercer Road, Townville. Has two kiddie rides, 3,000-square-foot maze, miniature golf, and playground. 814-967-3307.

INDEX OF MAJOR RIDES IN OPERATION IN PENNSYLVANIA

Roller Coasters

WOOD TRACK

Blue Streak, Conneaut Lake Community Park, opened 1937.

Hercules, Dorney Park, opened 1989.

Thunderhawk, Dorney Park, opened 1930.

Sky Princess, Dutch Wonderland, opened 1992.

Comet, Hersheypark, opened 1946.

Lightning Racer—Thunder and Lightning, Hersheypark, opened 2000.

Wildcat, Hersheypark, opened 1996.

Rollo Coaster, Idlewild and Soak Zone, opened 1938.

Jack Rabbit, Kennywood, opened 1921.

Racer, Kennywood, opened 1927.

Thunderbolt, Kennywood, opened 1968.

Phoenix, Knoebels Amusement Resort, opened 1985.

Twister, Knoebels Amusement Resort, opened 1999.

Leap the Dips, Lakemont Park, opened 1902.

Skyliner, Lakemont Park, opened 1987.

Comet, Waldameer Park and Water World, opened 1951.

Cyclone, Williams Grove Amusement Park, opened 1933.

STEEL TRACK

Little Dipper, Carousel Village at Indian Walk, opened 2001.

Little Dipper, Conneaut Lake Community Park, opened 1954.

Zyklon, DelGrosso's Amusement Park, opened 1987.

Laser, Dorney Park, opened 1986.

Little Laser, Dorney Park, opened 1987.

Steel Force, Dorney Park, opened 1997.

Talon, Dorney Park, opened 2001.

Wild Mouse, Dorney Park, opened 2000.

Woodstock Express, Dorney Park, opened 2000.

Joust, Dutch Wonderland, opened 1998.

Great Bear, Hersheypark, opened 1998.

Roller Soaker, Hersheypark, opened 2002.

Sidewinder, Hersheypark, opened 1991.

sooperdooperlooper, Hersheypark, opened 1977.

Trailblazer, Hersheypark, opened 1974.

Wild Mouse, Hersheypark, opened 1999.

Wild Mouse, Idlewild and Soak Zone, opened 1993.

Exterminator, Kennywood, opened 1999.

Lil' Phantom, Kennywood, opened 1996.

Phantom's Revenge, Kennywood, opened 2001.

High Speed Thrill Coaster, Knoebels Amusement Resort, opened 1955.

Whirlwind, Knoebels Amusement Resort, opened 1993.

Little Dipper, Lakemont Park, opened 1986.

Mad Mouse, Lakemont Park, opened 1991.

Toboggan, Lakemont Park, opened 1991.

Kiddie Coaster, Pocono Play Park, opened 1999.

Vapor Trail, Sesame Place, opened 1998.

Ravine Flyer III, Waldameer Park and Water World, opened 2000.

Kiddie Coaster, Williams Grove Amusement Park, opening not known.

Wildcat, Williams Grove Amusement Park, opened 2001.

Wooden Carousels

Albion Boro Park, manufactured between 1890 and 1990 by U.S. Merry-Go-Round Company, installed 1947.

Bushkill Park, manufactured around 1915 by Allan Herschell, installed 1993.

Carousel Village at Indian Walk, manufactured between 1891 and 1915 by Herschell-Spillman, repopulated with new wood horses along with antiques in 1991.

Conneaut Lake Community Park, manufactured in 1905 by T. M. Harton, several original figures replaced with new wooden ones in 1988, installed 1910.

DelGrosso's Amusement Park, manufactured in 1924 by Herschell-Spillman, installed 1924.

Dorney Park, manufactured in 1924 by William Dentzel, installed 1994.

Hersheypark, manufactured in 1919 by the Philadelphia Toboggan Company, installed 1944.

Idlewild and Soak Zone, manufactured in 1931 by the Philadelphia Toboggan Company, installed 1931.

Kennywood, manufactured by William Dentzel in 1926, installed 1927.

Knoebels Amusement Resort, Grand Carousel, manufactured in 1913 by Kremers Carousel Works, installed 1944.

Knoebels Amusement Resort, Kiddieland Carousel, manufactured around 1910 by Stein and Goldstein, installed 1976.

Peddlers Village, mechanism manufactured in 1922 by Philadelphia Toboggan Company, repopulated with wooden replicas in 1998, installed 1998.

Weona Park, assembled by William Dentzel in 1923 using machinery and figures carved between 1885 and 1917, installed 1923.

Dark Rides

The Pretzel, Bushkill Park, opened 1930s.

Devil's Den, Conneaut Lake Community Park, opened 1968.

Chocolate World, Hersheypark, opened 1973 (located outside front gate).

Gold Rusher, Kennywood, opened 1981.

Old Mill, Kennywood, opened 1901, rebuilt 1926.

Haunted Mansion, Knoebels Amusement Resort, opened 1973.

Wacky Shack, Waldameer Park and Water World, opened 1970.

Dante's Inferno, Williams Grove Amusement Park, opened 1985 (using older ride).

Walk-Throughs and Fun Houses

Barl of Fun, Bushkill Park, opened before 1930.

Confusion Hill, Idlewild and Soak Zone, opened 1984.

Noah's Ark, Kennywood, opened 1936.

Pirate's Cove, Waldameer Park and Water World, opened 1972.

Allotria Fun House, Williams Grove Amusement Park, opened 1972.

Log Flumes

Thunder Creek Mountain, Dorney Park, opened 1982.

Double Splash Flume, Dutch Wonderland, opened 1977.

Coal Cracker, Hersheypark, opened 1973.

Log Jammer, Kennywood, opened 1975.

Flume, Knoebels Amusement Resort, opened 1990.

Thunder River, Waldameer Park and Water World, opened 1996.

River Rapid Rides

Thunder Canyon, Dorney Park and Wildwater Kingdom, opened 1994.
Canyon River Rapids, Hersheypark, opened 1987.
Raging Rapids, Kennywood, opened 1985.

Splash-Water Rides

White Water Landing, Dorney Park and Wildwater Kingdom, opened 1993.
Tidal Force, Hersheypark, opened 1994.
Pittsburg Plunge, Kennywood, opened 1995.
Sklooosh, Knoebels Amusement Resort, opened 1997.

BIBLIOGRAPHY

Books

Adams, Judith A. *The American Amusement Park Industry: A History of Technology and Thrills.* Boston: Twayne Publishers, 1991.

Anderson, Norman. *Ferris Wheels: An Illustrated History.* Bowling Green, OH: Bowling Green State University Popular Press, 1992.

Bush, Leo O., and Richard F. Hershey. *Conneaut Lake Park: The First 100 Years of Fun.* Fairview Park, OH: Amusement Park Books, 1992.

Cartmell, Robert. *The Incredible Scream Machine: A History of the Roller Coaster.* Fairview Park, OH: Amusement Park Books; Bowling Green, OH: Bowling Green State University Popular Press, 1987.

Fried, Frederick. *A Pictoral History of the Carousel.* Vestal, NY: Vestal Press, 1964.

Griffin, Al. *Step Right Up Folks.* Chicago: Henry Regnery Company, 1974.

Jacques, Charles J., Jr. *Goodbye, West View Park, Goodbye.* Natrona Heights, PA: Amusement Park Journal, 1985.

———. *Hersheypark: The Sweetness of Success.* Jefferson, OH: Amusement Park Journal, 1997.

———. *Kennywood . . . Roller Coaster Capital of the World.* Vestal, NY: Vestal Press, 1982.

———. *More Kennywood Memories.* Jefferson, OH: Amusement Park Journal, 1998.

Kyrazi, Gary. *The Great American Amusement Parks.* Seacaucus, NJ: Citadel Press, 1976.

Mangels, William F. *The Outdoor Amusement Industry.* New York: Vantage Press, 1952.

Manns, William. *Painted Ponies: American Carousel Art.* Millwood, NY: Zon International Publishing Co., 1986.

O'Brien, Tim. *The Amusement Park Guide.* Old Saybrook, CT: Globe Pequot Press, 1999.

Reed, James. *Amusement Park Guidebook.* New Holland, PA: Reed Publishing, 1987.

Magazines and Newspapers

Amusement Business. 1961 to present. Billboard Music Group, P.O. Box 24970, Nashville, TN 37203.

Amusement Park Journal. 1979 to 1987. Amusement Park Journal, P.O. Box 478, Jefferson, OH 44047-0478.

Carousel News and Trader. 1986 to present. Carousel News and Trader, 87 Park Ave. West, Suite 206, Mansfield, OH 44902-1657.

Merry-Go-Roundup. 1975 to present. National Carousel Association, 128 Courtshire Lane, Penfield, NY 14526.

NAPHA News. 1978 to present. National Amusement Park Historical Association, P.O. Box 83, Mount Prospect, IL 60056.

Roller Coaster. 1978 to present. American Coaster Enthusiasts, 5800 Foxridge Dr., Suite 115, Mission, KS 66202-2333.

Selections from 1908 *Street Railway Journal,* in *Traction Heritage* 9, no. 4 (July 1976).

INDEX